Fo

KNOWING OURSELVES

Knowing Ourselves is one of three books in the *Foothold* series. Over the next 100 days you are invited to explore aspects of both God's character and your own, learning what it means to be human from many of the case studies found in the Bible.

Although *Knowing Ourselves* is ideal for use with the *Contemporary Version of the Bible* (CEV), it can be easily used with other modern versions of the Bible. In this copy of *Foothold* the CEV text has been quoted and in specific instances the *Good News Bible* (GNB) and the *New International Version* (NIV).

Set time aside and establish a simple pattern for using this book.

Enjoy your journey!

Scripture Union
Resources for Ministry Unit
PO Box 77, Lidcombe, NSW 2141 Australia

Prepared by Sally Apokis, Merryl Blair, David Cohen following a syllabus designed by Charles Sherlock
Editor: Rena Pritchard
Design and Layout: Allan Weatherall, Insight Graphics, Melbourne
Cover Photo: Allan Weatherall
Printed by Jenkin Buxton Printers, Pty Ltd, Box Hill
ISBN 0 949720 58 5

Foothold

PAGE

HOW TO USE FOOTHOLD

As you journey through life learning more of what it means to be human, you find you are also learning about the character of God. But to do this well you need to spend time with God who then becomes the yardstick for your actions, rather than human models.

The Bible provides us with a huge resource for learning about human nature. To reach our full potential as humans we need to listen to what God is saying to us through the Bible, rather than pretending it is telling us what we want to hear. Then we have to start allowing that message to *actually* impact on our lives.

Scripture Union has devised a simple four step method which many people have found helpful as they meditate on what the Bible says.

Prepare your mind and whole person to actively listen to God. *Knowing Ourselves* contains a variety of ways for this. You will gradually find the ones that suit you best. (See article on 'Knowing what God wants us to do' on page 28.)

Read the verses for the day. The passage will raise questions in your mind. You will find you are constantly surprised by how 'earthy' God is. How surprising to find that God is interested not only in your highs and lows but also the mundane aspects of your life.

Explore Think about what the passage throws up to you before reading the comments in *Foothold* for the day. For example,

- What is the main point?
- What does it teach about God — the Father, his Son Jesus Christ, or the Holy Spirit?
- Is there a promise, a warning, some special orders to obey or an example you should note?
- What fresh insight does the reading give about yourself, your situation or your relationships?

Allow time for considering one of these questions before reading the Explore section in *Foothold*. Jot down any thoughts or questions in a notebook. Use it as a journal to chart your reflections as you examine afresh the various aspects of being human.

Respond by taking your discoveries seriously. If you need to talk things through share your thoughts with a more experienced Christian or see if your Christian bookshop has a book on the particular topic. God wants to work with you. It is through your eyes, ears, feet, hands and lips that God is enabled to do some aspect of his work on earth. You have real choices — some better than others in God's view — but there is not always a single right course. What is most important in what God will tell you through the Bible and his Spirit is that he values your uniqueness and *will* share life's journey with you (Matthew 28:20).

Check point A

GOD'S VISION AND SIN'S REALITY

INTRODUCTION TO READINGS 1–10

These readings introduce us to some of the most important concepts in the Hebrew Bible. In Hebrew literature, the main point is usually found at the beginning, so what is contained in the first eleven chapters of Genesis is not there by accident as we shall see. All the Near Eastern cultures surrounding ancient Israel had creation stories. They grappled with the great human questions such as: 'How do we fit into our world?'; 'Why is work so hard, childbirth so painful?'; 'Why are men and women different, and how should they live together?'

The Hebrew people also asked these questions, drawing their answers from experience of God working with them in history. The early chapters of Genesis insist that God is totally involved in creation. Human beings are seen to be part of the wider picture, and given special responsibility to care with God for the rest of creation. And in an indefinable way, human beings, male and female together, are seen to reflect the very nature of God.

Part of being human is to make mistakes, as the stories of Genesis 3, 4 and 11 clearly show. The good news is that God's grace is equal to our mistakes, and new starts always follow the mess-ups!

Genesis 1 — 11 is often called 'Pre-history', telling the story of God's action in the whole cosmos before the call of God to Abraham to start a special people who are to have a special relationship with him. This 'Pre-history' comes first, to make it clear that God is first and always interested and involved with the whole of creation. All creation is 'good' in God's eyes, even in the midst of our human mistakes and failings. God always finds new ways for us to start again.

DAY 1: IMAGE MANAGEMENT

Imagine you are walking to your local shops. Think of who you pass, the different ethnic groups, the young, old, eccentric… Are *all these* made in God's image?

Genesis 1:26-28

Genesis declares boldly that God created the whole world. The culmination of God's communicating and creative activity occurred when 'God said, "*And now* we will make human beings; they will be like us and resemble us"' (GNB, 26). That we are like God, resemble God, are related to God stuns and scares us too.

But self-love, personal and media driven, can distort our perceptions. Sub-consciously we may relate to others as created equal by God only *if* they look like us, or fulfil current definitions of beauty as relayed through media images. Then for peers to take us seriously, image becomes critical. The nearest thing to Godlikeness might be the current 'designer' look complete with name brand sunglasses, joggers or roller blades, or a 'charity shop' look of sensible walking shoes and brown cardigans.

We need to move beyond 'image' to see that each person in a crowd reflects God's glory. The upwardly mobile 30 year old who has 'arrived' socially is *not* representative of God's likeness. The *fullness* of male and female identity includes the chubby baby girl from Ghana; the dirty and dehydrated boy from Central Australia; the Thai teenage prostitute; the homosexual emaciated young man dying of AIDS, covered in skin tumours; dear Grandma, deaf and blind, kept warm under her crocheted rug. All these are image bearers of God. While we argue about identity, pecking orders and prejudices, the writer of Genesis tells us clearly that human identity has its primary relationship *with* and *in* God.

Jesus, help me see your face in everyone I meet today. Amen.

DAY 2: ACCOUNTABLE TO GOD

Do you know any environmentalists? And do they get to tell their stories, ask for prayer, teach people songs at your church?

Genesis 1:26-28 (continued), Psalm 8

In an age of environmental concern, Christians have received strong criticism because of ideas that stem from this passage. Here the creation mandate says that human beings are to 'rule over the fish, the birds, and all other living creatures' and also, to 'have a lot of children. Fill the earth with people and bring it under your control' (26,28). As a result Christians have borne some of the blame for the ecological, environmental and cultural degradation of the earth.

However, these words were directed to *all* people, not specifically to the Jewish audience of the time or Christians later in history. They spell out for all time that the welfare, cultivation and care of the earth is the responsibility of *all* humans. In the drive to harness, capture and control resources, a good relationship to the earth and all that is in it has gone missing. Instead of using God's *mandate* of power and authority over creation to give and sustain life, this power has so often been misused throughout history. This has resulted in oppression, imperialism, destruction and degradation.

Seek out laments or litanies for your church to use to express sorrow to God for situations where we have endangered or destroyed the goodness of God's world. What opportunities are present in your local community for you to be active alongside others in loving care and concern for the environment?

Thank God for 'Green' groups whose members dedicate their lives to caring for the earth justly and lovingly, which is what God originally called us to do.

DAY 3: A TABLE OVERFLOWING

Recall a Greek or Italian party, Jewish or African feast where the table overflows with food that is not carefully rationed out. Then think how a refugee might pray, 'Give us our daily bread'.

Genesis 1:29 — 2:3

Only after describing the lip-smacking smorgasbord of food that God provided for both people and animals to enjoy does the writer note that the whole universe is now complete (31)! Then it is siesta time (2:2) for God! A wonderful insight into God's personality, that God intended you, me and everyone else to eat, enjoy and rest.

When the refrigerator is empty we crave food. After too much work or partying we miss a night's sleep. But how insignificant is this 'deprivation' compared with the gross malnutrition suffered by millions or the exhaustion endured by refugees and those trapped by war? Such suffering is wrong — it flies in the face of God's loving intentions for humans. God's provision is like that of a favourite aunt who slips an extra cream cake onto our plate at dinner time before tucking us into bed. Everyone should experience such care. Later books of the Old Testament and parts of the New Testament pick up on images of food, feasting and God's rest to describe the kingdom of God, culminating in the life of the Messiah. They remind us that God wants everyone fed and rested, living a life filled to the brim with good things.

God, your desire is for us to enjoy the feast. We are thankful for the food we have.

You have provided abundant food for all yet we live in a world of unjust food distribution. Make us active where we are to ensure all are fed, cutting down on food wastage and composting any leftovers.

You are the bread of life, Jesus.

Amen.

DAY 4: FROM DUST TO GRANDEUR

'From the stars our bodies have come, under the stars we all are one, now into deepest night we go. Alone, but not alone.' (Children's lullaby) The chemistry of our bodies is similar to that of the stars. And the same person who created the stars also made us, intending all of us to live in intimacy with both Creator and creation. Awesome.

Genesis 2:4-9

Genesis 1:1 — 2:4a gives a slightly different view of the creation story to Genesis 2:4b-25 because it is telling us different things. Pretend you and others were able to watch God as he created the earth and all that is part of it (note Proverbs 8:22 ff.). How might each person interpret the process? Some would draw or sculpt, compose a poem or write a newspaper account. Those who express themselves through music and song would describe the experience in a variety of ways. The rest would watch in awe and fear, speechless, capturing the 'moment', perplexed at what it all meant.

Within the space of a few days I attended the birth of my niece and buried a dear friend. The stark realities of life and death were placed side by side. There is something unreal and miraculous about birth, as we see a newborn babe coming into the world. Despite our knowledge of biology we wonder, 'wow, where did *you* come from?' Yet lowering my friend's unpolished pine coffin slowly into the brown and ochre earth, we *knew* where we came from. Each death marks time for us. In witnessing the end of a life the earthiness of our humanity is starkly presented before us.

Write a prayer or poem, taking the time to reflect on your life as part of creation, 'Dust to dust, ashes to ashes…'

DAY 5: A JOB TO DO

Did you hear these creation stories as a child, and have the images changed for you?

Genesis 2:10-17

The one God put in charge of the Garden of Eden represents all humans, who are expected to share responsibility for caring for the earth (1:28). God re-emphasises this call to care, delivering the first 'but' to humans, placing boundaries on them. And these first restrictions relate to food!

Is God fickle? After offering a banquet (1:29,30), why suddenly exclude the fruit from this particular tree? Can a fruit have the power to enable us to distinguish between right and wrong? We need to understand that the Hebrew Genesis creation stories were like stories from other primitive societies, making sense of the awesome. Handed down orally, they gave explanations to countless generations about good and evil and how plants and people came about. Powerful mystery was always an element. They tell theological truths but were never intended to represent simply historical or scientific events. Trying to establish a date for when the first Adam and Eve existed, searching for evidence of a serpent or the location of the Garden of Eden and so forth, is not the point.

As the heirs of God's revelation to Abraham and Sarah, Moses and Miriam, the prophets and the later revelation in Jesus, these Genesis stories are *our* foundation stories, telling us how things came to be and are in relation to God. And in case we feel superior, we too desire to sneak away from the good life God has made for us, and seek to dwell in the dark places of sin and death.

Pray, read further and talk about the meaning and significance of this story with other Christians.

KNOWING OURSELVES

What does it really mean to be human? One key to our understanding is our ability to grow to know ourselves more fully. This comes through reflecting on our place in the world and on how our life experiences have affected us.

We are not always aware of how our own worldview shapes our attitudes, practices and relationships. Like all books, *Foothold: Knowing Ourselves* has a worldview, in particular one that comes out of a biblically based Christian faith. Its views on what it means to be human stem from that perspective. The 100 readings contain only a small selection of the Bible's teaching but this will give you an overview of some of the heights and depths of being human.

The second process that helps define us, our particular life experiences, are largely determined by our families and social setting, our genetic inheritance, where and in what period we live, our community language and what opportunities come our way or are denied us.

CHECK YOUR BEARINGS

On your journey through these readings, you are invited to test your own experience against the witness of the scriptures. The Scripture Union format will assist you to explore and assess your own worldview. You will discover ordinary people who find themselves catapulted into great responsibility or asked to make a difference to their circumstances. Laid out are the high points of human potential along with gross failures where the consequences of sin are presented for all to see. We learn that, though made for eternal glory, we all can become stuck in the mire of sin. You will be surprised at how many facets make up human life.

TRULY GOD, TRULY HUMAN

Examining the material as a whole, you will see how the Bible holds together twin truths about Jesus Christ: that as the unique son of God he is fully God and at the same time is fully human. It is hard for us to grasp that Jesus was 'exactly like God' (Colossians 1:15) yet also 'became one of us' (Hebrews 2:14-18) except in sin (Hebrews 4:15).

The Bible points us to the reality that it is through the life, death and resurrection of Jesus Christ that we see most fully reflected what it is to be human. And in Genesis 1:27 we learn that we are actually made 'in the image of God', something almost beyond our understanding. What a privilege, what a responsibility!

Knowing then that we are made in this same God's image, how do we go about learning more about the person, character and nature of God? And in the light of that knowledge, how then should we live?

Taking risks with God

We do not learn much about what it is to be human through book knowledge, even though other people's reflections add insights to our own. We learn through living and experiencing life, by taking risks, 'having a go' as we step out in faith, sometimes making mistakes. And when we do make mistakes, there is nothing so bad that we can't share it with God. After saying we are sorry (repentance), we can move on, humbler and wiser. Our lives are not always pretty, but we have been given the potential to work with God's Spirit to become fully the person God intended us to be. Through living and making choices, we gradually learn more about ourselves and what we were created to become.

An intimate relationship

The scriptures and creation speak to us about God and about God's character. And as we spend time meditating on the scriptures, and in talking and listening to God (prayer), we will learn more and more about God and about ourselves. How we envisage God says a lot about ourselves. If we imagine God as impersonal or an abstract power, we keep ourselves distant in our relationships with others, or become uncaring about the consequences of our actions or words. But as we allow ourselves to be open to God's voice, we ground our faith in the scriptures and find there a God who is anything but an abstract, remote entity.

OUR BROTHER, JESUS CHRIST

To find God we are instructed to first look to Jesus Christ (1 Corinthians 12:1-3; John 1:1-18). In Jesus we find a person who is passionate, fearless, able to be angry when necessary yet tender and compassionate, patient, articulate but able to be still, a brother, a friend, one who *chose* to come and live with us. It is through Jesus that we pray, our sins are forgiven and we are guided. Everything that exists involves the activity of Jesus Christ.

We learn about Jesus through his Spirit, who is also divine. It is through the Spirit that God becomes involved in every nook and cranny of our lives (1 Corinthians 2:10). How often are you aware this is occurring, or that you allow God into not only the major parts of your life but also the peripheral parts that also make up who you are?

OUR OWN FATHER

Jesus referred to God as his own Father. As disciples of Jesus we too are invited into God's intimate circle as family, where we will find him to be generous, fair, forgiving and faithful. How then can we think of God as remote and uninterested in us? When we pray, it is not to a distant God, but in and through Christ, in the Spirit, the Trinity, a close and warm family. 'God is love' (1 John 4:16) and it this image of God that we need to hold. Only as we obtain a full and rounded image of God can we go on to become full, rounded people.

NEW DIMENSIONS

Television has opened up to us the whole spectrum and variety of human existence. We see humans attaining peaks of excellence in so many different categories, along with images of degradation and horror. We can look back through history and see how our understanding of God and of what it means to be human has developed. Many of us today now see what it is to be fully human quite differently to those of a generation ago. Then we described ourselves as *mankind*, now our image encompasses a fuller view of *humanity*, as we have included the female dimension alongside the male, to give a more complete image of human life.

We hope that this *Foothold: Knowing Ourselves* will give you the opportunity to look afresh at yourself and at how you see the world and experience life and to review this in the light of the scriptures. Then we hope you will be able to better integrate your faith with your place in society along with your accompanying lifestyle, and be bound more intimately to God as Father, Son and Holy Spirit.

DAY 6: MALE AND FEMALE

'A dog is a man's best friend?' Can this *really* be true?

Genesis 2:18-25

Men and women instinctively know that their lives are bound up intricately with one another. No matter how a particular society is shaped, there are many situations where women and men have to function in biologically defined roles. And new life cannot happen unless men and women perform their biological roles as male and female.

This story tells us in a straightforward way that the separate male and female identities need one another. From one, the male and female identity is spawned and then drawn back again into one, making a circle of completion. In marriage, the two identities become one. The orderly, safe pattern is like a Celtic knot, intertwined, meaningful and beautiful to look at.

But because in modern society there is so much interference with this pattern, in both social and technological practices, we need reminding that there is a normative pattern. Today, when there are many different kinds of families and relationships, it can become easy to forget that male and female identities are intrinsically bound together. 'Male-ness' and 'female-ness' have an equal share in what it means to be human; their separate male and female identities find unity in marriage. That does not mean that the shared path will always go smoothly. A lot has happened since creation. But the big picture still has much to teach us.

Pray and think about all your relationships with men and women. Is God encouraging you to seek reconciliation, to offer encouragement, to give of your time to a particular person, or the courage to begin to trust and unfold your real self to another?

DAY 7: SHIFTING THE BLAME

'The trouble with normal is it always get worse.'
(Bruce Cockburn)

Genesis 3:1-13

Sometimes you wonder if God knows what is good and bad. And you question God's ethics, especially when reading parts of the Old Testament. Take Holy War. Can you really understand this issue with both head and heart? What is so bad about humans knowing the difference between good and bad?

After the wedding it is not long before disagreements threaten marital harmony. It is easy to blame your partner, denying your share of blame and wrongdoing. What have we in common with Adam or Eve? Poor Eve. She is judged severely in this account of how sin entered human experience. Because Adam failed to accept responsibility for his behaviour, Eve is blamed, and women have borne the consequences of this incident throughout Christian history.

All sorts of women-hating behaviour has been condoned because only Eve was blamed for this dual effort. Here the *two* act like children caught stealing sweets although what occurs is far more serious than petty stealing. Trust has been broken. By their active pursuit of wisdom the two sever their trusting relationship with God.

The ancient Hebrews viewed this quest as akin to desiring God-like status. But imaged like God, we are not God! Humans have always struggled with this temptation in their relationship with God — we are to be *children* of God, not to *be* little gods. This story of sin and snakes teaches us about the relationship between who we are and what we do.

Dear God, don't let me be lulled into a false sense of security about sin. Shine light on the darkness in my life, freeing me from sin's power.

DAY 8: FOR YOUR OWN GOOD

While listening to meditative music, bring to mind a difficult part of your life, present or past.

Genesis 3:14-24

Consequences arise for man, woman and snake. The snake slinks away, an enemy. Women must now endure painful childbirth, oppressed by husbands yet ensnared by desire for them. Men too suffer — no longer enjoying earth's abundance as a gift, but constantly working to produce a living. If only we could stop the video of life, rewind to where things were going well, then 'freeze frame' the image. However, life isn't like this; our actions prevent us from going back.

After eating the fruit, they now know the difference between right and wrong (2:9, 3:7), with consequences for them and all people forever. Yet does God withdraw from parenting? No. It is as if God put on his gum-boots and walked in the Garden, first clothing then disciplining the children, acting as mother *and* father. God's response to their disobedience seems harsh, but unless kept from the tree that gives life (2:9) they will enter a state of endless sin. Banishment marks a new stage of the dynamic relationship between humans and God. Through relocation and displacement people are realigned and chiselled into creatures God relates to and works with as his purposes for them are fulfilled.

Lord God, we are sons and daughters of Eve and Adam.
We desire all and seek to have all.
We are tantalised by all that glitters in our society.
Forgive us for taking from where we shouldn't.
May your Spirit constrain us like a Mother hen with wings around her young, so that sin is kept at bay and Jesus may be known.

In him we pray, Amen.

DAY 9: MURDER MOST HORRID

'...One life with each other. Sisters. Brothers. One life.
But we're not the same.
We get to carry each other, carry each other.
One. One...' (U2 Achtung Baby.)

Genesis 4:1-16

Reading this passage in English conveys little of the force of the original Hebrew. The language is confronting because the word 'brother' is repeated many times. The story appals and startles us, yet we are made of the same stuff as these two siblings, and thus open to the same failings.

Family relationships bring mutual obligations of duty, honour, commitment and love. We should seek always to behave responsibly towards parents and siblings, not seeking to avoid our duty to care for them. And in looking out for one another, we should try to protect, guard, respect, honour and love each person. Family members should not kill each other.

With levels of domestic violence rising, it is hard to understand why some people lash out and harm the very ones who are their responsibility. Is it jealousy? One child may resent another's personality or abilities. A parent may favour one of their offspring over another. Anger management may be a problem. Is there no trustworthy person to unburden to, seek advice from? Have we forgotten how to say sorry? What prevents us from admitting our failings when confronted with them? Pride?

We may not commit physical murder, but we can commit murder in our hearts (Matthew 5:21-22), destroying the love and acceptance we owe to family members.

God is a God of peace and reconciliation. If you have experienced or observed family violence first hand, try now to share these situations and individuals with God.

DAY 10: FOR YOUR OWN GOOD

When people tell jokes, have you noticed the puzzled look on those who understand little English? Do you feel excluded when you are in a group speaking a language you don't know?

Genesis 11:1-9

Is this a story about division or dispersion? God could be seen here as vindictive, spiteful and petty, as he gently mocks the people's collective effort to urbanise, fortify and glorify human endeavour. The impetus to move to Babylonia and build was clearly not God's initiative so from where did it come? Was it from an enthusiastic, 'I can do anything, be anything' group, ready to take on the world?

This bold attempt to build a metropolis reaching towards the sky may have been aimed at self-glorification. Their advanced technological skills may have duped them into thinking they could create something better than the Creator's gift. In seeking to make a *name* for themselves they seem to be trying to tantalise or tease God.

Or perhaps they were seeking self-protection, wanting now to stay put, rather than move around. Did this then undermine God's creative desire for them to be fruitful and fill the earth? Was God mocking their puny efforts (7), pressing them to learn they were human, not God?

The point of the story is that languages become the means of creating divisions between peoples, and this story provides an explanation for why there is a dispersion of languages and nations. The story suggests that God placed limits on how human fulfilment was to be achieved.

Many modern technological advances far exceed this ancient tower building exercise. In what ways have we benefited? And where might we have become too smart for our own good?

GOD'S WAY FORWARD

Check point B

INTRODUCTION TO READINGS 11–18

'But God has shown us how much he loves us — it was while we were still sinners that Christ died for us.' *(Romans 5:8 GNB)*

This gives the essence of the whole message of the Bible! Life's journey is one of ups and downs, with movement towards and away from God. This is so for God's people as a whole, and for individuals.

The letter to the Romans addresses part of this journey. A minority Christian community is struggling with what it means to belong to God in a difficult political climate. Jewish Christians expelled from Rome in 49 AD were able to return there in 54 AD, after the death of the Emperor Claudius. The small group of non-Jewish Christians left behind had grown and now the church was faced with the task of making two culturally different groups into one community. This was proving to be difficult. Paul reminds them of what they have in common: they are all created human beings, all have sinned, all are in need of God's grace which is offered to each of them through the death of Jesus Christ.

Returning to Genesis again, the next readings take us back to our common beginning and our shared need for God's grace. As each human disaster unfolds it is matched with an unexpected offer initiated by God for an undeserved chance to renew their relationship with God. The rainbow, symbol of the promise given to Noah, demonstrates God's love and concern for all creation. The symbols of new names and the rite of circumcision confirm the promise (or covenant) given to Abraham. These symbols demonstrate the presence of the 'cosmic' God in ordinary lives. The God of history still journeys with us today. God's grace continues through our 'highs' and 'lows', giving today's people new starts, new status as members of God's family.

DAY 11: THE SIN THAT MARS AND SCARS

What do you like about yourself; what would you want to change?

Romans 5:1-11

Moving from the earthy narrative of Genesis to Paul's reflection on how Jesus makes sense of everything, Paul may talk more to your situation than the shadowy characters of Genesis. *'We have been put right with God'!* Still sinners, we are included and comforted, but our status has changed. Now *'we have peace with God through our Lord Jesus Christ'* (1,GNB)

From Chapter 3 on in the Genesis stories, we observe the entry of the sin that mars and scars. Jesus would have absorbed these stories too (2). But when we learn that God *allowed* his only son to be slaughtered for us (6,8), our image of what a father should be is shattered. What father would allow his son to be beaten, tortured, spat upon, mocked and humiliated for the sake of one human being, let alone billions of people? Confusing, difficult, yet Paul calls it kindness (20) and love (5,8). Why did God send Jesus to die for us, and how did this bring peace and reconciliation between him and us (10)?

To understand God's ongoing relationship with us, read *Foothold: Discovering God* to learn more about Jesus, the Father and the Holy Spirit. Reading this story in isolation offers us relief for we learn that Jesus dealt permanently with the sin that separated us from God. However, for a balanced view of God we need to look further in the Bible — or we may see just a son-hating father. Try Colossians 1:9 — 2:19 for a start. In turn, what we read here rests on the condition of 'faith', another story!

Write a prayer to thank God for the coming of Jesus in your life.

DAY 12: BEHIND SIN SALVATION WAITS

Contrast the backdrop of partying and drunkenness at Christmas with the carols that encourage us to *'Come let us adore him... Christ the Lord.'*

Romans 5:12-21

Sin surrounds us. It comes through events big and small, within and without, and through people. There are occasions when even respectable people fail to respect and care for the property and feelings of others. All of us have at times taken the easy way out, not thinking of the consequences of our actions. Or, we deliberately go ahead with something even though we know it could hurt others.

Paul knows about sin. He has seen its effects in people he knows and loves, both in his society and in himself. We too know sin from the inside; we see and feel it. Sometimes we perpetrate sin, at other times we are its victims. Sin is at work in society's structures, ever present, bringing death.

Paul talks about Adam, Moses and Jesus: he discusses Adam in relation to sin, Moses in relation to God's ancient laws, and links Jesus' name with God's gift of acceptance and peace. The Law came into existence to contain and deal with sin (13, 20), but is unable to bring life. Jesus alone brings life (21).

The sweet sound of *'Joy to the world, the Lord has come'* at Christmas reminds us that we can experience a breath of new life through God's gracious gift in Jesus, rather than allow ourselves to be destroyed by the violence that sin brings.

Reflect on parts of your life and circumstances where you know sin has visited in a big way. Can you see where God's laws and God's grace are able to provide freedom?

DAY 13: RATIONALISING OUR BEHAVIOUR

'When the wild-eye dogs of day to day come snapping at your heels... When your hands are full of thorns but you can't quit groping for the rose... When the sun comes up an enemy and nothing gives you shade... Lie down, and take your rest in me.'

(Bruce Cockburn, 'Dart to the Heart', Sony Music, 1994)

Romans 7:9-25

What happens when you chat with friends over coffee about business ethics, personal moral issues, the ground rules for society? Does the chatter turn to tension? Do you find Christian views at odds with community opinion?

As we struggle with envy, pride or other sins, we rationalise our behaviour. We develop different coping mechanisms, condoning some situations so as to ignore or give scant attention to the process of wrestling with wrong.

Paul reflects here on the struggles Christians face. Christians know that grappling with sin is real and unsettling and we worry in the process. It is healthy to take a periodical personal stocktaking, but don't work on this alone... it's too hard. Becoming part of a small group or confiding in an older Christian is helpful. The sharing of burdens, 'confession' as it is sometimes called, is an age-old Christian practice (James 5:17). Confession helps us to identify the problem, deal with it and receive God's forgiveness. This, in turn, may bring about real healing. Remember that Jesus is present with us in the struggle.

Are you making your Christian life harder by trying to do things alone? To put things in perspective, share any struggles with your minister or another Christian.

DAY 14: FRESH HOPE

What sustains you and gives you life?

Genesis 4:25 — 5:2

A new babe is born to our ancestors, a sign of renewed hope after an appalling incident reflecting total family breakdown. Note the timing of this apparent coincidence: 'About this time people started worshipping the Lord' (25,26). And despite the disaster of human sin that preceded this birth, God reaffirms his original intention for humans, they are created 'to be like himself' (5:1) and given his blessing and a distinct name (2).

'Blessing' is viewed as old-fashioned yet we seek it through status, lusting after consumer goods and the trappings of today's materialistic world. Yet if we seek such lifestyles, we show no understanding of the true nature of blessing. To the first families of Israel who received God's blessing, blessing *and* curse were an accepted part of their relationship with God. Everyone knew that all of life — family, government, and religion — was infused with the reality of God's presence. They experienced and understood God's intentions and desires for them. In receiving God's love they responded by living within God's favour. This was God's blessing.

If we seek 'blessing' through materialistic personal goals, and try to create our own destiny, we will soon find how inadequate this is. Jesus says blessing comes not to those who have everything but to those who continue to be faithful in spite of lives of struggle, suffering or drudgery. Those who know what they lack (Matthew 5:2-12) receive the promises of God's salvation; they will inherit the coming kingdom. This commitment gives us fresh hope.

Meditate on Matthew 5:2-12. What are the important things in being human? Now make a checklist of things that should have a stronger place in your life.

DAY 15: I CAN SEE A RAINBOW

Do you remember drawing rainbows as a young child? What did they say to you then? What do they say to you now?

Genesis 9:8-17

If you are around children you may have noticed that depictions of Noah, the ark and all the merry little animals have become fashionable and are imprinted on many accessories for children. Noah stencils are available for painting friezes on children's bedroom walls. There are Noah curtains, bedspreads, cushions, mugs, toys, candles and tapestries. You could fit out your entire home with items fine and frilly, all with Noah motifs! When you read the whole Noah story, you find all is not pretty. So why depict it on domestic furnishing fabrics? The story seems out of place in today's sophisticated society.

What are these stories of Noah about? Is the story of Noah and his ark just a cute children's story? The stories mark out the ebb and flow of curse and blessing: after devastating curse blessing follows. Note the striking repetition of words at the conclusion of the Noah story (9,11,13,15,16,17): 'solemn promise', 'I promise', 'I will remember'. God is binding himself to an eternal promise. To underscore this, God causes an eye-catching reminder to arch across the sky for all to see and recall this special promise. It will reappear in the sky from time to time. God is depicted here with human characteristics: God sends, remembers, sees, makes promises. Limited by our humanness, we need such concrete expressions as rainbows to be able to understand and picture God. These descriptions lead us into the core of the story: God stands by his solemn promise: never again will the earth or its people suffer total devastation.

Can you see now why the rainbow is a symbol for various justice ministries? Thank God for them.

DAY 16: LAUNCHING OUT

What keepsakes do you have to remind you of significant events in your past or your family's? Spread them out and spend time meditating on what they mean to you now.

Genesis 11:31 — 12:3

As you read the Bible, God often singles out a person to do a specific task. We call this a 'call'. This story has all the classic characteristics of a 'call' initiated by God. Abram, the 'father' of the Hebrews, Christians and Muslims is singled out. 'Hey Abram, leave everything you know, everything that is the world to you — family, relatives, home. Then come with me to a place of my choosing. Don't worry about what place; the place isn't important, you won't even have heard of it!' Would a sane person say yes to a call like this?

We have already seen hints of God encouraging scattering in our earlier readings. And we have also seen how God seems intent on blessing members of his earthly family. And what a blessing! Not only is it for Abram, his family and his descendants, it is for everyone on earth! And it is no miserly blessing.

What does all this mean for us? God's participation with humanity is neither random nor an abstraction. God deliberately chooses, initiates, offers, promises and actually requires us to participate willingly with him. God's participation in our lives is confronting. We are asked to go to places, peoples and spaces we may not care for. We will not be alone for we are assured of the comfort of the presence of an 'on the move' God, a God who journeys with us.

Thank you God for telling us you are present with us through your message to Joseph when baby Jesus was coming: Immanuel, God is with us (Matthew 1:23).

DAY 17: NEW NAMES, NEW NATION

Reflect on the meaning of the name God has given you or the one you would choose for yourself.

Genesis 17:1-5, 15-16

Twenty four years after God's initial promise, again Abram is promised the world. Much has happened — famine, a move to Egypt then back to today's southern Israel. When their promised son (Genesis 15:4) does not eventuate, his wife Sarai takes matters into her own hands, and so an unsavoury episode in family relations unfolds. The resultant 'eternal triangle' involving Abram, Sarai and Hagar does not leave this supposed hero of God blameless.

Again God repeats the promise (1,2). Abram bows in customary response. Note that the promise is given to *both* Abram and Sarai. Having nearly lost Sarai in Egypt, experiencing apparent sterility and old age, the couple *will* now become the father and mother of many, many descendants. And those descendants, even powerful ruling descendants, will have a relationship with God.

Then comes the outward sign of God's promise. Both are to have new names — Abram is to become Abraham and Sarai, Sarah. Have you noticed how God seems to enjoy playing with people's names? Jacob became Israel, Naomi became Mara, Simon became Peter, Saul became Paul. Until recent times, when women and men joined religious orders, they took on a new name at their consecration, marking the beginning of their new life. Names are important in the Old Testament. 'Abraham' in Hebrew sounds like 'father of many nations'; 'Sarah' may mean 'princess'. New relationships, new standings, new promises are marked by the giving of new names.

Thank God for your name and your new identity in Jesus.

DAY 18: THE CUTTING EDGE

Does circumcision mean anything to you? If you have a Jewish friend ask them about its importance.

Genesis 17:9-14

Changing names is one thing, surgically removing sensitive body parts another. God makes concrete his promise to Abram and Sarai by changing their names. God *seems* to get off lightly (4-7). For humans the stakes are higher — circumcision seals the promise for Abraham and his male descendants, and will demonstrate their faithfulness. The ancient rite of passage receives new meaning, the painful and bloody sign providing physical evidence that they are 'in' with God.

New mothers hearing the anguished cries of their beautiful babes, fathers and the men holding them down as flesh is cut away, each share the infant's pain. They cannot fail to grasp the cost of their intimacy with God. Nowadays, circumcision is carried out in hospital settings using anaesthetics. This deadens the rawness of this distinctive practice. In the original intimate ceremony we see something of God's passion for his covenant people who acknowledge, 'we are yours'. While God's people remained faithful to the initiator of the sign, the symbol had meaning.

The New Testament takes up the issue of circumcision in a radical way (Romans 2:25-29; 1 Corinthians 7:18-19; Galatians 5:6), moving the symbol beyond surgery to touch the heart. When we belong to Christ, whose blood was shed for us, we gain spiritual freedom. But faithfulness and obedience to Jesus is not trivial, passive, unemotional. It requires everything of us, even blood, anguish, tears, pain and courage.

Our hearts we give you,
Our whole body we give you.
Our feelings, emotions,
Our thinking and remembering we give you,
All of our selves we give you Lord Jesus. Amen.

KNOWING WHAT GOD WANTS US TO DO

Do you know your star sign? And do you ever read your horoscope?

Many people dabble in astrology, and so numerous newspapers and magazines publish horoscopes. This is evidence of our great human desire for guidance and longing to know the future. We want to make the right decisions about our time and money, our work and friends. And, if we're honest, we're also afraid of what might lie ahead. We want to avoid danger, mistakes, unhappiness and accidents. The attraction of astrology is that it claims to know our personality and fate; but at its heart is fear.

When we belong to Christ, we step out of fear and superstition and into love. Love is the perfect antidote to fear. We discover that God made us and knows us completely. In Jesus we have a Saviour and Friend who has defeated all the powers of darkness and evil, including death. We also have the Holy Spirit within us, who can help us see the truth — with the wisdom and peace of Christ.

There is no magic formula for finding God's will, but some simple principles apply in every situation. The most important thing to remember is that God *wants* us to walk in the right direction. God will never fail us, never break a promise, never deceive us, will prove closer than a brother or sister and be more reliable than a best friend.

So what are these simple principles?

- **Be open and honest with God.** Read Psalm 32 for help in starting from where we *are* rather than from where we would like to be. God is holy, and we must begin by confessing our sins and asking his forgiveness. Then the lines are open for us to communicate freely with God, because we aren't hiding any guilt, shame or anger.

- **Keep God's law.** This may sound rather strict and legalistic, but God's law is designed for our freedom. We're free *not* to steal, lie and envy. We're released from our obsessions with 'other gods', be they possessions, people or pastimes. But if what we *think or feel* God wants us to do means breaking one of the Ten Commandments, then it is *not* God who is guiding us.

● **The church is the place where together we live the life of the Holy Spirit** — there we find our unique place among God's people, and how we are to serve in God's world. The Holy Spirit will guide us, promised Jesus (John 16:13).

FULL HUMANITY ONLY IN JESUS CHRIST

INTRODUCTION TO READINGS 19–27

Way back in our first reading from Genesis 1, we saw that human beings were created to reflect God. By the time we have read these next readings, we might feel that humans were created to reflect *Days of our Lives*! What a case study of dysfunctional families!

The interesting thing is that God chooses to work with these less than ideal people. And as we read we will often see ourselves and our situations reflected in the biblical story. Some of these characters are hard to relate to, because they are often unsympathetic, even downright unpleasant! It is especially hard to read these stories if we see ourselves or our particular situation in them. *But* God is there in the darkest moments, and these moments have to be lived through.

In case we feel stuck in the soap opera, the readings from John's Gospel, Philippians and Hebrews remind us that there are other ways of being human. It is Jesus who brings us back to reality, to what it *really* means to be human. These passages stress that Jesus experienced all the struggles we experience (he was not allowed to cheat on life!). In the early church there were suggestions put around that Jesus only pretended to be human and to suffer. This idea is firmly rejected by the New Testament writers. Why we are able to become fully human is *because* Jesus 'gave up everything and ... became like one of us' (Philippians 2:7).

The writer of Hebrews (and other New Testament writers) often uses 'family' metaphors to speak of our relationship to God (brothers, sisters, etc). There is hope for our less-than-ideal family relationships, because full humanity in Jesus restores and reconciles beyond the sphere of the individual.

DAY 19: A FIGURE OF FUN?

Dear God, help me to learn from the hard, confusing and unpalatable parts of the Bible, not just the comforting parts.

Genesis 9:20-27

The near total destruction of the human race has done something to Noah. These are the only recorded words of Noah — the first written record of one human cursing another — a curse upon his grandson! Why does Canaan receive the punishment when his father Ham is in the wrong? What annoyed Noah so? Would you place a curse on your child or grandchild? Are we so different to Noah?

The Bible often uses short crisp sentences to describe disapproval, rather than giving lurid details. Why did this saintly man get drunk so soon after receiving the rainbow promise? These early biblical stories show humans responding to God's goodness in fluctuating ways — acts of obedience and unacceptable behaviour. Ham's actions were totally out of place in terms of family respect, honour and dignity: finding his father drunk and naked he makes fun of him. Perhaps there is an unstated darker side — did Noah's inebriation lead to the common side effect of sexual misconduct?

We see Shem and Japheth's concern for their father — their response is described in detail. This tragic story catalogues how one family got things wrong. Coming just after the rainbow and God's solemn promise it strikes an ominous chord. What *is* the story ... morning glory?

O God of the stars and the night skies
May your light be coming through thick clouds this night
On me and on everyone
Coming through dark tears
On each one in need and in suffering. Amen.

[J.P. Newell, *Each Day and Each Night*, Glasgow: Wild Goose Publications, 1994, p. 32, used by permission]

DAY 20: UNREALISTIC EXPECTATIONS

In what ways are your views of women in society and the church different from your parents' generation?

Genesis 29:15-30

As a modern person did your temperature rise as you read about the injustice of this scheming father exchanging his own daughters to exploit a man? How does this fit with the Christian's knowledge that all are made equal in Christ (Galatians 3:28)?

Laban and Jacob demonstrate that the beauty myth extends far back in time. Beautiful Rachel with her sparkling eyes and good figure is viewed a better catch than dowdy Leah. *Of course* Jacob was in love with Rachel — what healthy male would not be! And he does get the lovely Rachel in the end, with the servant woman Bilhah (and later Zilpah, 30:9) tossed in as well!

In these early biblical stories of our forefathers (the 'Patriarchs') the man always seems to get his woman. The promise of God finds fruition only through the birth of children. As in many cultures today, women then found security, status and significance only through their roles of wife and mother.

We may want to wrestle and fight against this ancient way of life. So many women throughout the world still suffer injustice and exploitation within similar patriarchal structures as Leah and Rachel's. Rethinking and changing these patterns is a difficult challenge. But if we can do something to change such situations, even in small ways, we should work towards this. Later in Israel's history, the prophets condemned unjust social, political and religious structures. Jesus, through his life and work found a different way to relate to women and men.

Knowing all, both male and female are equal in Christ, does this affect your response to the scriptures?

DAY 21: FAMILY COVER-UPS

Think of a saga or funny story from your family history. If you were to include it in your family crest what symbol would you choose?

Genesis 27:1-29

Each of the stories about the male patriarchs in Genesis — Abraham, Isaac and Jacob — fails to mention what is owed to the matriarchs. Sarah, Hagar, Rachel, Leah and Rebekah are significant for much more than their child producing capabilities. It turns out that the real power centres are found in these behind-the-scenes bedroom dramas of domesticity rather than the public and political lives of their males! The Bible unselfconsciously relates the earthy realities of life, yet many Christians continue to surround the Bible with a puritan 'tsk tsk' attitude, which the world loves to parody.

The stories reveal something of the power of these women, who often use trickery to help their husbands. Rebekah moves the men in her life around like pieces in a game of chess. Success comes through the use of food, whose power is only equalled by sex! At the birth of her sons, Rebekah received special words from God — the younger Jacob, not the older twin Esau, would become the father of many nations (25:22,23). Rebekah became a co-worker with God. Who understands love or how God chooses people? There seem to be elements of serendipity and mystery here. What sort of God are we dealing with here, who weaves into history the human frailties of deceit, manipulation and sexual politics?

Dear God, reveal gently to me areas within my family needing reconciliation and patching up. Give me courage and strength to initiate ways to change what can be changed and accept without bitterness what cannot.

DAY 22: SIBLING RIVALRY

'Envy, jealousy, malice and pride — they must never in my heart abide!' (from a popular old chorus) Have these created problems in your extended family? Who is still hurting?

Genesis 29:31 — 30:24

Polygamy was part of the normal structure of the ancient world and although discouraged by Christian missionaries it has been very much a part of African life. In this passage, polygamy is not condemned but it does not ignore the complications it creates for families. Today it is again an issue in countries like Rwanda, because so many males there have been murdered.

What is the underlying problem in this story? Is it that Jacob has a favourite wife, rather than that he has two wives? And are matters complicated because the women are sisters?

Modern 'blended' families experience some of the struggles found in this ancient blended family. What is it that attracts one person to another? Even in a committed relationship no person is immune to attraction to another person. What strategies do you use to cope with these situations? It is not always easy to assess what God would have us do. And, like Jacob, humans spend a lot of time undoing the consequences of unrestrained emotions and preferences.

Jesus, we struggle to be faithful to you.
We struggle to be faithful to our marriage partners.
We struggle to be faithful to our families.
We struggle to be faithful to our friends.
Be in the struggle,
Help our weakness,
Strengthen our commitment,
Love us in our frailty,
We ask in your faithful name, Amen.

DAY 23: DARK SECRETS

'Everybody hurts sometime...' (pop group, REM)
What wounds are you willing to bring to God?

2 Samuel 13:1-21

An insatiable world media market shows our collective voyeurism. The sexual exploits of Royalty or Hollywood provide weekly soap opera material for magazines and TV. Even when we know the meaning of words like dignity, discretion, invasion of privacy and propriety, these values seem to be from another world. Yet at heart we would prefer that celebrities could lead a normal life.

In Samuel, another Royal family is enmeshed in tawdry sexual exploits', even incest. And sadly, this family has contributed to our Jewish and Christian heritage. Recorded here in the family history of David, the family the longed for King of Kings descended from, is this blunt and brutal story. Amnon's evil intent is described frankly with no attempt to gloss over the details. He deceives Tamar with food, using trickery similar to Rebekah when she and Jacob stole Esau's birthright. Another male colludes with Amnon, enabling him to rob Tamar of her virginity and innocence. Not condoned then, sadly this behaviour still occurs.

A whole range human activity is disclosed here. 'As the story unfolds, the two males move between protecting and polluting, supporting and seducing, comforting and capturing' Tamar (Phyllis Trible). In turn violence exposes hatred. What do *we* do with such a story? What do *you* do with such a story?

I bring my mixed emotions and confusion to you, O God:
We cannot whitewash the darkest of horrors, O God.
Our tears, our anger, our fists, our why seem futile.
Jesus, you know the anguish, you experienced it.
You know freedom. Come into our suffering and free us. Amen.

DAY 24: WORD ALIVE

Why on earth would God send a baby to teach us about God? Does it make sense to you?

John 1:1-18

John is teaching us an important Christian reality, although it is hard to understand it all. In his description of Jesus as the Word of God he forges links with the beginning of Genesis. The talking, communicating God who spoke then and brought creation into being by his Word, now births a son who communicates God with us. Jesus *is* the image of God into which we are made and John's gospel begins with describing this reality. As you read the whole gospel this human Jesus will gradually unfold. We come to see him as the means of God's communication, 'the bread of life', 'the good shepherd', 'the door', 'the way'... Jesus' life encompasses all the goodness God intended for us at the beginning of creation.

Some call Jesus 'the human face of God' because one aspect of God is that God has embraced humanity. God did not merely pay a visit to earth or let us know he was here through sending a fax, making a telephone call or even using the Internet. God in Jesus did not *pretend* to be human while still being God. God embraced our actual nature, coming to us in human form. God's dignity is not so 'precious' that he has to be protected from the less savoury realities of living in this world. We know this because his Son was not protected from these.

How are your senses? Are they dulled, swamped, exploited and oppressed? Ask God to help you find ways to understand this message that gives life and frees you. Share your current reality with him. Allow him to be real to you, to become 'flesh', alive.

DAY 25: TRUE HUMANITY

'It takes a lot of humiliation to learn a little humility.' Does this ring true with you?

Philippians 2:1-11

How preoccupied we are today with who we are and with our rights. Forever protecting ourselves from potential threats to our well-being, we feel people or institutions are out to get us. 'Who's getting the best out of this deal?' 'Who's benefiting most from this relationship or situation — am I being used?' Once where seeking help though conflict resolution might have brought shame, we now seek 'postive outcomes' through it.

We are told that for society to ultimately benefit there must be winners and losers. Downsizing a business or moving it off-shore to survive or maximise profits is a case in point.

Paul up-ends this perspective. Jesus became the loser so that we could benefit, giving up everything to become like one of us, even dying on the cross (7,8). But as a result he became the pinnacle of creation (10,11). For us to share life with Jesus we need a very different lifestyle to the 'me first' generation. Life is to be shared with others (2). Yet asked to imitate Christ's humility and obedience, possibly facing death (5-8), who is strong enough to follow in Jesus' footsteps?

No one. It is only through God's Spirit that we can become united, unselfish and aware of others' needs (1). This enables us to live together in harmony (2) without jealousy, aware of the importance of each person. We need to learn to care for others as much as ourselves, and to 'think the same way that Christ Jesus thought' (3,4).

Thank you God for what you have done for me in Jesus. Help me to seek out other Christians more, learning to play my part as a member of a Church community.

DAY 26: THE SPITTING IMAGE

Sixteenth century radical reformer, Thomas Muntzer wrote: *'Thomas Muntzer will pray to no mute God, but only to a God who speaks.'*

Hebrews 1:1-4; 2:10-15

The Book of Hebrews presupposes some knowledge of the Old Testament regarding the Jewish priesthood and sacrificial system. In Chapters 1 and 2 the writer tells us that God has spoken to us before and is now speaking through his son, Jesus (see especially 1:1,2). Chapters 3 to 10 look at what it means for us that Jesus is our high priest and what his sacrifice means while Chapters 11 to 13 spell out the implications of this.

Today's verses tell us specifically that to find out about what and who God is we need look no further than his son. Jesus is God's 'exact likeness' (3, GNB), yet shared our human nature. When we understand and appreciate what Jesus' life, suffering and death has achieved for us (2:9,10) we become part of his family. Jesus accepts us then, even going as far as calling us his brothers and sisters (2:11). No social, cultural, political or religious barriers prevent us from entering into this closest of family relations with him. All that matters is that we believe and have faith in who Jesus is.

If you think back to the earlier passages in Genesis and in John that we have read, can you see how some of the themes intertwine with these in the book of Hebrews? Creation is there, the relationship of God and Jesus, and God's answer to human sin. As you read right across the Bible you will gradually see how often these big themes re-occur.

Read these words from Hebrews again — out loud. Then form them into a prayer to God.

DAY 27: TEMPTED LIKE US?

Think about some difficult personal situation you have faced. And how you encouraged and supported a friend through a dark patch?

Hebrews 2:16-18; 3:12-13

From what you already know of Jesus, was he fully human, fully God or both? Is our experience of being human different from his? Did Jesus have a head start on us? This passage says this is not so. In a later chapter, faith is described as the hope of things not yet seen (11:1). It is hard to imagine that Jesus could have been tempted, yet it states here that Jesus *was* tempted like us. Unlike us, he resisted temptation. Does that give you some sense of assurance that God knows your struggles and is able to do something about them? Don't be tempted to play God's role when you are confronted with situations bigger than you can handle. We all want to help then but what should you do?

Affirmation of Faith:

I believe in Jesus Christ, Son of the one God, maker and sustainer of earth, sea and sky.
Born of Mary's womb, Faithful to the God of Abraham and Sarah,
Jesus healed the sick, served the poor, and proclaimed heaven on earth.
Condemned by the religious, Crucified by the state,
He died but transformed even death and rose to life everlasting.
He blessed the disciples with his Holy Spirit and sent them forth, east and west, north and south.
I commit myself to Jesus. To one another as brothers and sisters and to his mission in the world in the grace of the Holy Spirit. Amen.

[*The Iona Community Worship Book*, Glasgow: Wild Goose Publications, 1991, p. 44, used by permission.]

Check point D

GOD'S CONCERN FOR THE WHOLE OF LIFE

INTRODUCTION TO READINGS 28–36

There are great, cosmic themes running through the Bible. There are also many accounts of God's involvement in the small, seemingly insignificant details of human life. The Psalms reflect all aspects of experience, from the great joy and peace experienced in the beauty of creation, to the darkest depths of despair. Psalm 139 is typical, showing that God is present in all experience, and that all experience, good or bad, belongs before God in worship.

Similarly, the letter to Timothy and the book of Leviticus, in different ways, celebrate God's involvement in the details of life. The letter is practical advice to a young Christian on making every-day decisions according to Christ-like standards. Leviticus is concerned with holiness: keeping life ordered and pure, to reflect the holiness and purity of God. Chapter 15 is part of a section dealing with the issue of what is clean or unclean. It probably poses more difficulties for the modern reader than almost any other part of the Bible! However, it shows that faith is not simply to be 'spiritualised', but belongs to every sphere of human life, however mundane.

The main purpose of working out the 'clean' from the 'unclean' was to protect the holiness of God from being defiled by the unclean. Many Gospel stories show that Jesus turned this concept upside down, as we can see in Mark 5. When Jesus touches someone who is ritually 'unclean', rather than the 'holy' being defiled, the 'unclean' is made pure, acceptable and whole.

Once again, God works in unexpected, surprising ways to bring life into dark places.

DAY 28: INSIDE KNOWLEDGE

'Everybody likes to see justice done on somebody else.'

Bruce Cockburn

Psalm 139

One of the hardest questions to answer is how far intimacy with God goes. Should we be so close and pray for something as trivial as finding a car park in a crowded place? Should your parking problem be as important as the reality that 40,000 children will face death tomorrow through starvation?

God does not ignore the big or small questions of life as the writer of this Psalm knows. No corner of our thoughts escapes him (1). The psalmist feels protected (5) but also knows one cannot hide from God's Spirit (7) whether escaping to the heavens or to the 'world of the dead' (8). God has known the writer intimately since conception (15,16). And even in danger or confronted by enemies, the psalmist knows that God will 'lead me in the way that time has proven true' (19,22,24). The psalmist does not ask to be removed from the danger but expects God to be present.

Some say the most dangerous people in history and in the world today are the well intentioned. If this is true then the most dangerous Christians in the world are those who have no doubts that God is looking after them. They assume, implicitly or explicitly, that if others do not seem to be looked after, the fault lies within the person. The noted cosmologist, Paul Davies, chastises those who believe in a 'guardian angel' type God. To really practice the art of believing in a God who loves and cares for you, is to continue to have faith against all odds when it does not appear that you are looked after or cared for by God.

Break up this Psalm into seven sections. Pray one section each day of the week.

DAY 29: GREAT STUFF

'All truth is God's truth. All beauty is God's beauty.'
Do you feel comfortable with this statement ?

1 Timothy 4:1-10

Why do some Christians always seem to oppose each new trend in contemporary culture? Once 'rock 'n roll' was viewed negatively, and before that, ballroom dancing. There was a rumour about the song 'Stairway to Heaven' — if played backwards, something unspeakable could be heard. But today, even at Bible colleges, you will see students sporting T-shirts promoting all sorts of things, even punk heavy metal bands, and no one seems to bat an eyelid. How then do we determine what is good or bad in everyday culture?

This reading tells us everything is good (5). This does not mean that anything goes for Christians, nor that we try everything on offer just because it is there (4,6,7). No, the challenge for the Christian is to identify what can be received with thanksgiving and prayer (4,5). In a pluralist society it is difficult to deny that other religious views or customs also promote goodness. Instead of always speaking out against the things we believe are no good, it is better for Christians to witness through their lives about God, the author of all that is good, using words only when appropriate. And, we should actively encourage worthwhile things in our society or neighbourhoods (10). We need to discern and choose our vocation carefully, and how we spend our time and our income. And discernment is also needed to counter false religious claims in teaching and in lifestyle (1-3).

Thank God for the good things in your present life, especially the ordinary ones, using short sentences. Become confident about acknowledging who is the source of the good things you are sharing.

DAY 30: PURE EMISSIONS

What matters do you feel uncomfortable talking about with friends? With workmates? In social settings? Think about your reasons.

Leviticus 15:1-18

Is there nothing the Bible will *not* talk about? Leviticus talks frankly about intimate matters few of us discuss even in private. It is easy to dip into passages like this to make fun of the Bible, showing how boring and irrelevant it is.

Since Leviticus was written, our knowledge of science and the way society is ordered has changed much. The original context and importance is lost to us. This manual reminded the Israelites how they should conduct themselves personally so the harmony between God, the world and God's people was preserved. This desire for harmony explains its strong themes of holiness and purity. Every aspect of human conduct, from birth to death, from rising to sleeping, was covered in books such as Leviticus.

In primitive societies, impurity, uncleanness or pollution resulting in skin disease, genital discharges, nocturnal emissions or menstrual flows, were believed to flow from uncontrollable processes. These emissions disturbed the harmony of life although they were *not* seen as evil or sinful in themselves. Leviticus 15 provides an orderly way to control the inexplicable. As we can explain these emissions in physiological terms, it is tempting to laugh at our spiritual ancestors. We would benefit more by directly relating every aspect of our lives to God, the outstanding message of Leviticus. It encourages us to live totally integrated lives, not dividing aspects of our daily lives into the sacred and secular, but acknowledging God in every part.

Does this reading challenge you to re-order your priorities in relation to God, the world and others? Review the whole of your daily life, from morning to evening, Sunday to Saturday.

DAY 31: LIFE BLOOD

Have you ever given blood at a Blood Bank? How did you feel? Did it have any religious significance for you?

Leviticus 15:19-28

Not long ago a friend and I came across a workshop entitled 'Honouring the menstrual blood'. We decided it was not for us. While other societies treasure many of the rites of passage of life, Western society has dissociated itself from most of these. Another friend grew up in Papua New Guinea and lamented such things. There, in a public celebration, the local people killed the fatted pig to mark the commencement of a girl's menstruation. In Western Christianity, traces of misguided notions about sexuality remain from the past, implying sexuality is sinful and therefore dirty. So menstruation is still rarely discussed in public or in mixed company.

But biblical Israelite religion sees sexual relations within marriage as one of the highest, purest and holiest human activities. The constraints they placed around menstruation resulted more from a lack of scientific understanding than anything else. So menstrual uncleanliness was treated similarly to a man's semen emissions. Symbolic purifications by ritual immersion were prescribed for men and women alike. We need to see these ancient writings in their original cultural, historical and religious settings or we will be trapped into comparing apples to oranges.

It is good that the Bible gives meaning to and honours the significance of *everything* to do with male and female life. With blood we live, without it we die. Our bodies need the rhythmic pumping of our blood to be healthy. Women especially experience the ebb and flow of life-giving blood. Jesus experienced the shedding of his blood. He knows what it is to give life.

Can you talk openly with other Christians about *all* life matters? Do men and women respond differently?

DAY 32: WOMEN'S BUSINESS

Who is outcast, a pariah, untouchable or unloved in your world? Bring each to God.

Mark 5:22-43

Two females — a girl, an insider, dead; a woman, an outsider, living death. Imagine the bustle and distress as these stories unfold: Jairus begging Jesus to come and touch his dying daughter; Jesus diverted by the touch of the woman. Unworried, Jesus takes his time and the young girl dies. Continuing to her home he wades through the wailing crowd. Then, taking the dead girl by the hand, now an unclean corpse, he surprises everyone when she rises, well.

Note the parallels between the dead girl and the bleeding woman. Any woman with continuous menstrual bleeding was totally outcast in those times (cf. Leviticus 15). If young when her problem arose, her family and any potential husband would abandon her and she would stay childless and friendless in a living death. If older, she would lose her status in the community and the company of her family. To afford to consult all those doctors she must have been wealthy (26). Now healed by Jesus, she can be restored to a place in her family and society. (Some Bible translations have Jesus call her 'daughter' — placing her in Jesus' family.)

The twelve year old girl, on the verge of adult womanhood, is also restored to her place in society. As the child of a significant religious person, Jairus'daughter had a place in society, with access to a good life. Jesus heard her loving father's desperate plea as she lay dying. Two unclean women were touched by a loving, saving, healing God and given life, identity, place and meaning within society. Smashing and destroying all that binds, Jesus brings astonishing freedom to all who trust him.

Re-read this story. What barriers, isolation, fear, sectarian behaviour and homogeneity contribute to living death in your community? Seek Jesus' power to transform these.

DAY 33: A PROMISE FULFILLED

Read Psalm 113. Imagine God as a great King, exalted over all nations. Now imagine God walking into your house, caring about all the tiny details of your daily life.

1 Samuel 1:1-20

What a graphically drawn portrait of domestic life! It depicts the grief of a couple desiring children but unable to have them. Today this grief is still shared by many couples and their families, each experiencing keenly a personal sense of loss. In ancient Hebrew society there was the added social pressure requiring them to produce a son. A barren woman could never play a full role in society if unable to produce the children vital for passing down the family inheritance. The pain experienced by Hannah was made more intense because of the cruelty of Elkanah's other wife (6). (Note that polygamy was then an accepted 'family' pattern.)

Eli the priest was dismissive of this woman pouring out her grief to God. He never considered that the Lord of the universe could be interested in her petty problems.

Yet the priest, in responding to Hannah's explanation of her behaviour hints at God's likely response: 'You may go home now and stop worrying. I'm sure the God of Israel will answer your prayer.' (17)

The God of Israel has already shown he is deeply concerned with the 'under-dog'. He led the slave people out of Egypt and gave them their own land. Now we see that God's concern extends into the smallest details of people's lives, for 'the Lord blessed Elkanah and Hannah' (19) and Hannah gave birth to the longed for son.

Imagine God is present with you as you go through your daily routine. Practise talking to him about your small concerns. Learn to enjoy his companionship.

DAY 34: A SACRIFICIAL PROMISE

Read or recall the story of Abraham and the boy Isaac (Genesis 22). In your imagination, see the event from the sidelines. What feelings arise in you?

1 Samuel 1:21-28

Is this passage a climax or anticlimax to the chapter? From one perspective the 'happily ever after' ending of our last reading receives a set-back here. From another, it restores a satisfying balance as a vow is fulfilled.

From where we sit we would like to see this poor mother enjoy her longed for child but she appears to have enjoyed his company for only a few short years. However, Hannah seems to accept the situation gladly, so grateful is she for God's gift of a child. She sees it as perfectly fitting that she should give the child back ('lend' him back, is a correct translation of verse 28 — Samuel is a pun on 'lend'). God kept his word, so Hannah is willing to keep hers.

As with the story in Genesis 22, greater themes are present in this story than what appears on the surface. The fulfilment of promises is to lead to great things for Israel. For Abraham, it results in a line of descendants that grow to become a 'mighty nation' (promised by God in Genesis 12). For Hannah, the willing sacrifice of her son will provide Israel with a great leader who is to mediate for them with God and take them into the period of kingship. And, on a more personal level, Hannah's rival will never again taunt her about her barrenness.

Meditate on the words of Matthew's Gospel: 'You're a good and faithful servant. I left you in charge of only a little, but now I'll put you in charge of much more.' (Matthew 25:23) Do you see these words applying to your life?

DAY 35: A TALE OF TWO FAMILIES

Pray 'The Lord's Prayer' slowly (Matthew 6:9-13), meditating on each section.

1 Samuel 2:12-26

If the last reading left you feeling sorry for Hannah, you can see here that she was probably much happier than Eli. What a contrast between the two families! Eli, the main priest at the important sanctuary at Shiloh, is anguished by the behaviour of his sons, and confronts them (22-24). The position of priest was vital to Israelite society. They were responsible for teaching the people about God, so when priestly leaders led hypocritical lives they failed God as well as those in their care.

Hannah loaned her only son to God and does not feel sorry for herself. She is able to visit him yearly, so is not totally deprived of his company. On this visit, Eli blesses the family and promises more children (20). The barren woman is to be blessed with numerous children. And Samuel, the child she gave to God, 'grew up at the Lord's house' (21). What an honour!

Next we are given a glimpse of future events. Eli's family is doomed, because they have failed to take their God-given responsibilities seriously (22-25). Samuel, on the other hand, is headed for greatness: 'The boy Samuel continued to grow and gain favour with the Lord and with men.' (26, GNB) Parents cannot be totally responsible for how their children turn out, but we can imagine the grief of Eli, a faithful servant of God, as he watches his sons make choices that will lead to their death.

Think of different members of your family. What sort of feelings come up? Bring each person before God now.

DAY 36: SHATTERED DREAMS

Recall a time of disappointment. Read Psalm 42 and pray along with the psalm writer.

1 Samuel 4:10-22

The doom foreshadowed for Eli's family is played out now. This tense, tragic scene sketches for us a lonely, blind old man and a pregnant wife waiting for news of the battle. They embody all who have waited in dread for news of loved ones.

The entry of the messenger, who runs into town dressed in the classic signs of mourning — clothes torn, dust on his head — tells us that the news will be bad.

This family tragedy is a microcosm of the national tragedy soon to shatter the confidence of the people of Israel. Loss and death on the personal front helps us understand the wider national loss. A pregnant woman learns she has lost her husband in battle, then her father-in-law, just as she is to give birth to a son. Her grief parallels Israel's tragedy when the ark, symbol of God's presence with Israel, is captured. In naming her son Ichabod, 'No glory', on her deathbed, she embodies Israel's grief.

Great themes in the Bible are always connected to ordinary lives. God's plans for his people were frustrated by the sin of Israel's leaders (represented by Eli's sons). This is not some great cosmic battle fought far from human circles but concerns ordinary people whose lives are shattered because of other people's faithlessness. From earlier parts of this story we know that God is already working to pick up the pieces, and that Eli is part of the on-going story of Samuel. The bigger picture continues.

Read today's newspaper, looking for signs of hope (*good* news). Thank God for the way he continues his work in the world using the lives of ordinary people.

E Check point

LIVING IN THE FACE OF SUFFERING

INTRODUCTION TO READINGS 37–48

The book of Exodus contains a story that is foundational to the faith of Israel. In the story of Moses, we see the formation of the great leader who took a group of slaves out of Egypt, led them through years of wandering in a desert, and made it possible for them to come to a land of their own. More than this, though, it is the story of a God who heard the cry of an enslaved people, was filled with compassion for them, and established them as a new nation based on mutual care and respect, rather than on 'might is right'.

Beginning with Israel's oppression, we see how the courage and faith of several ordinary women paves the way for Moses' survival. Moses is the means by which Pharaoh's might will be thwarted, allowing the eventual entry of the people of Israel into the promised land. As these readings show, Moses had no easy task. We are introduced to the difficulties of leadership as we read Moses' story, and we can sympathise with his frustration, anger and despair at different stages. As we come to see, being called by God for a special task involves pain and hardship, as well as achievement. We can also see that liberation is not a once-only event, but something that needs to be worked on life-long.

Along with the Exodus readings, we see these themes expressed in various ways as faithful people try to cope with suffering. The Book of Job is a magnificent play that struggles with the problem of innocent suffering. Similarly in the Psalms, the question that arises is 'Where is God?' in the midst of life's tragedies. No neat answers seem to result from these questions. Life is often simply tragic. However, God is still the liberating God of the Exodus, so hope and comfort can only lie in conversation with God. Above all, these readings reflect the importance of honesty in our conversations with God. We can talk to God about the frustrations, tragedies, problems, as well as the good times.

DAY 37: BRAVE WOMEN

Shout praises to the Lord!
He is good to us, and his love never fails.
Everyone the Lord has rescued from trouble should praise him,everyone he has brought from the east and the west, the north and the south. (Psalm 107:1-3)

Exodus 1:15-22

When God called Abraham to follow him, he promised him that he would be the father of a great nation (Genesis 12). Escaping to Egypt because of famine Abraham and his family endured many set-backs. Now, the descendants of Abraham and Jacob have survived and their increased numbers make up a significant part of the population. Pharaoh wishes to keep the traditional structure of Egyptian society, so to maintain the wealth and privilege of the favoured ruling class he must keep the growing Hebrew population enslaved and oppressed (9-11). Again God's promise is under threat. The Hebrew people, far from experiencing the promise of God, are victim to a deliberate attempt to weaken and eventually eliminate their race (16).

However, the bravery and cleverness of just two people, the Hebrew midwives, helps carry forward God's plans for Israel. Their response is a model for living under oppression. Lacking power and privilege as slaves and women, they are among the least important in Egyptian society. Using the only power they have, choosing to be 'faithful to God' (17), they refuse to obey Pharoah. Depending only on the meagre resources of their faith and natural wit, the actions of these lowly women frustrate the will of the mighty Pharaoh.

A poster reads, 'God, nothing will happen today that you and I can't handle together!' Think of times when you have felt powerless and unimportant. Where is God for you in these times?

DAY 38: TWO MORE BRAVE WOMEN

Bring to mind again the two women in Mark 5 (Day 32).

Exodus 2:1-10

Life is precarious for the Hebrews, especially for a male baby (see Pharaoh's final order, 1:22). The Israelites live with danger in Egypt and the danger now focuses on one person, the baby Moses. Once again, he is saved through the skilful planning of a woman, this time Moses' mother. The description of her careful preparation of the basket shows us how tenderly she cared for this healthy baby boy (3).

The 'star' of this story is the baby's sister. Following the examples of the Hebrew midwives and her mother, she breaks out of her lowly, powerless position. She uses her natural intelligence and bravery to save the baby. Not only is the baby saved, but a link is created between the child's real mother, the child and the Egyptian princess. The mother is even paid to care for her own child!

Among the ruling, oppressing Egyptians is a woman who chooses to act with compassion towards those less fortunate. The relationship which develops between this sympathetic, powerful woman and the brave, powerless women of Israel sets in motion mighty events. These lead in turn to God's greatest action in the history of Israel: the Exodus (or 'liberation') from Egypt. Once again, through the actions taken by particular human beings, God's promise moves towards fulfilment.

How do you see other people? Who are your allies when under oppression? Spend time reflecting on whether there are sections of society or other races that you have 'written off'? How do you think God sees these people?

DAY 39: IDENTITY CRISIS

Where do you feel most 'at home'? Write down some of the reasons you feel you belong there.

Exodus 2:11-22

Little wonder that Moses experiences a classic 'identity crisis'! Born into the slave caste but brought up as part of the ruling class he enjoys the power of the second while retaining sympathy with the first. When events begin to pile up he is forced to choose between the two situations. He can keep on pretending about who he really is, thus maintaining his privileges as a member of the ruling class or, he can seek to find his true identity, which will mean having to identify with the hard life of his people. How does Moses respond to his dilemma? By choosing the common way out — he runs away.

But he cannot run away from the real problem because he still feels dislocated and without roots, even naming his first son after his feelings (22; *Gershom* sounds like the Hebrew for 'an alien there').

Running away may help for a short while when we need breathing space to think. But as with Moses, we eventually learn that the only way forward is to work out who God wants us to be. The process of finding an answer to this question is not achieved without pain. Here we see Moses on the brink of a life-journey which will be difficult and painful, but he is not expected to walk alone.

Have you 'run away' from certain situations? Or, have you faced tensions in your 'class' experience? Bring these to God now and ask for help in dealing with your past and present situations.

DAY 40: TOUGH CALL

Sit quietly and concentrate on your breathing. As you breathe in, feel God's peace flood your body. As you breathe out, let your frustration, anger and other negative feelings flow out.

Exodus 5:1-23

Moses has come back to Egypt, sure of God's call to him, and fired up with enthusiasm for the job God has sent him to do. Now he hits cold, hard reality as his first attempt to negotiate with Pharaoh fails.

Pharaoh does not know God, and is not interested in what God wants. Moses and Aaron argue their case forcefully but Pharaoh makes no concessions and introduces harsher work practices.

Pharaoh's tactics seek not only to destroy Moses' first attempts to carry out the job God wants him to do, but aim to make his ongoing task even harder. By setting Moses an impossible task, Pharaoh attempts to destroy his leadership and crush the spirit of the Hebrews. When set quotas are not achieved, the slave leaders are punished. Picture their anger and helplessness as they find themselves trapped in a highly organised, inhumane system! Not unexpectedly, they take their anger out on Moses. He must have felt like a pricked balloon with his mission blocked so soon.

Where did Moses go? Straight back to God. He questions the meaning of his whole mission. Forcefully he points out to God that not only has God failed to liberate the people, but he has made their lives even harder.

Have you found your Christian journey difficult and discouraging at times? Moses was not afraid to tell God that he was angry with him. Neither need we be afraid. Tell God about your anger and frustration, and allow him to take part in all aspects of your life. Now think of a country where there is oppression and resultant suffering. Does this story give you insight into how you can pray for the community of sufferers?

DAY 41: LIBERATION

Recall an experience where you were part of a group that was without hope and powerless, then imagine God as your place of refuge in this threatening situation. Now read Psalm 91:1-4 if you have the time — and let the word speak to your situation.

Exodus 14:5-31

In our last reading, Pharaoh said 'Who is this Lord and why should I obey him?' (5:2). Today we see God complete Pharaoh's education. The numerous plagues sent by God against Egypt have certainly attracted Pharaoh's attention, but still he fails to understand the point of the plagues. The might of God (might *is* something Pharaoh understands) may be convincing but the essential, liberating nature of God is beyond his comprehension.

Up to now this very nature of God is something which is also beyond the comprehension of the Israelites. Verses 10-12 show them as a group of people still captive to their fears, unable to grasp the freedom offered to them. They need the encouragement of Moses, also struggling with his own fears: 'Do not be afraid. Stand firm and you will see the deliverance the Lord will bring you today' (13, NIV). By the end of the chapter, there is no doubt that not only is God mighty, but that God chooses to use might on behalf of the powerless to bring about their liberation.

The task of liberation, as shown in the last words of this chapter (31), depends on the initiative and power of God. Liberation is usually carried out in partnership with ordinary human beings who, despite their fears, continue to trust God's guidance, as Moses did here.

Do you pray for seemingless hopeless world situations where liberation seems far off? Pray for them now. Then thank God for the instances of dramatic changes of circumstance you recall.

DAY 42: WHY DO BAD THINGS HAPPEN

What explanations have you heard others use to explain suffering? How do you explain suffering?

Job 7:1-10

The Book of Job is a study of meaning in the face of suffering. Many people today, including some Christians, believe that God sends suffering as a punishment for sin. This common perception, shared also by ancient people, is even found in parts of this book of the Bible.

But the writer of Job cannot accept this common view that suffering is sent as a punishment. What is his explanation for why bad things happen to good people? At the beginning of the book we are told that Job is completely blameless. Yet he is subjected to enormous suffering (see the first two chapters) which he refuses to accept is a result of sin. He clings to his honest belief (which has come from his observation of how things actually are) that life is, quite simply, very difficult.

This speech tells us how Job actually feels at this moment: there is no pretence that life is fine, no attempt to impress anybody, even God. Job feels that life is little better than slavery, and as far as God is concerned, gone in a flash.

Although this may seem a negative view of God and life, Job is telling God exactly how he feels. Still, even in the midst of these feelings, Job cannot imagine a life without God as a conversation partner.

How have you responded to difficulties in your life, 'Those things that hurt, instruct' (Benjamin Franklin)? Look back over your life. Think of a hurtful experience that led to growth? What still waits for healing? Share this with God.

DAY 43: GONE MISSING

Read Psalm 139:1-6 or the whole Psalm if you have time. Underline any words or phrases that stand out for you.

Job 10:1-15

'Big Brother is watching you!' This phrase, from George Orwell's book *1984* has often been used to express the feeling of living under a totalitarian regime.

Yet this is precisely how Job experiences God at this moment! The nightmarish image of a God looming over us, watching for the slightest little slip, ready to swoop down in wrath to punish, seems to be at the centre of this cry from Job. God's presence is neither comforting nor sustaining to him, but rather oppressive (3) and destructive (8). Job is the more hurt and bewildered by this experience because in the past he has always found God to be comforting and sustaining (12).

The most important point in this very difficult picture of Job's experience of God seems to be that God's presence is still there for him. Two of his friends have spent a great deal of time speaking to him but Job has found still that the only person worth talking to is God. If he cannot get an answer from God, no one else is able to help. The worst pain is not that of physical suffering, but the spiritual anguish of feeling rejected by God. Despite this, Job demonstrates his questioning faith by refusing to give up the conversation with God. Nor should we when in similar circumstances.

Read Psalm 139 again. How do you experience God at the moment: like Job, or like the psalmist? Both these feelings are present in the Bible. Both are found to be legitimate human responses to God at different times of our lives.

DAY 44: LIFE'S FRAGILITY

Plan to spend ten minutes in the garden or nearby park. Look closely at a small plant or flower. Observe the delicacy of its structure, how intricately and beautifully it is made. Thank God for his care for small parts of creation such as this plant or flower.

Job 14:1-14

Job continues his complaint against the oppressive presence of God. Part of his frustration now is the feeling that because life is so short we should at least be left alone to live it, without worrying about God breathing down our necks all the time!

There is a refreshing honesty in Job's speech. He faces up to the reality of mortal existence. His friends are trying to use words to wallpaper over the facts of life: sorrow and suffering, grief and death. Job insists that life be met head on with no pretences. Human beings are mortal, so why pretend otherwise? In the depths of despair, Job still displays a courage which shows up his friends' refusal to live in the real world.

Our society displays a similar refusal to live in the real world, with its emphasis on staying young and beautiful. We push illness and death into institutions where they cannot offend our eyes or force us to admit to our mortality.

The writer of Ecclesiastes also accepts the fragility of human life, suggesting that the wisest course is to live 'in the moment', rather than to spend our lives wishing for what we don't have. Accepting the human condition and learning to enjoy the life given to us can bring us peace.

List three things you love most in life: tastes, sights, smells, sounds, touches and three puzzling things. Spend time imagining the joy or frustration that each one brings you and share this with God.

DAY 45: WHERE ARE YOU, GOD?

When do you feel most alone? Is this a good or bad feeling? Imagine yourself without any family or friends.

Job 23:1-17

Our last three readings have shown us a Job oppressed by the sense of God's ever-watching presence. Now when he wants to meet God face to face he cannot find him anywhere!

Job insists on a faith which does not deny the difficulty of his life. It has led him to a point where he thinks that if only he could present his case before God and plead his innocence, God must respond favourably because God is just. For Job at this point, real faith cannot pretend that everything is going well between himself and God. Real faith insists on pushing at the relationship until he gets an answer, any answer from God.

However, the writer of the book knows that the life of faith is not so easy. When we ask for an answer from God it does not necessarily mean we will get an answer, or the one we want, at the time that suits us.

The paradox of Job's relationship with God is that God is beyond Job's control. Job cannot make God go away, neither can he demand God's presence and answers whenever he wants them. God still refuses to live within our boxes, and will continually break out of any restrictions we try to place on him. When God does appear to Job (chapters 38 — 41), we realise that he was listening all along. Job's awareness of God's presence, even though that presence is beyond his understanding, finally provides him with the meaning for which he has longed.

Read Psalm 73:21-26. What part speaks most strongly to you at this moment? Try re-writing it in your own words as your prayer to God.

DAY 46: HELP ME GOD

A popular saying, 'It's not the gale but the set of the sail...' suggests viewing tough times and pressure from a different perspective. Does this help?

Psalm 56

Over one third of the Psalms are laments, prayers which cry to God from various situations of need or hurt.

This psalm gives words to a feeling all of us experience at times: life is unfair; people are out to 'get us'. The urgency of the language takes us into the psalm writer's hurtful situation. Whenever someone spreads lies about us, trying to do us an injury, we too can share the writer's fear and outrage. The enemies' weapons are difficult to combat: rumour, lies, slander.

The psalm moves from a cry for help to the very human demand to 'get them back'(7), then settles into a more serene mood from verse 9 on. Although it seems the problem has not actually gone away, the psalmist, now assured of God's presence, is able to recognise that what people say is not really important.

God does not whisk us out of hard situations but gives us resources to work through them, learning and growing in the process. This does not mean we should not ask for his help. The writers of the Psalms show us that to lay our problems out before God is an act of true worship, in which we allow God to take part in every aspect of our lives, both good and bad.

Life brings problems. No problems would mean no life. What is your biggest difficulty at the moment? Ask God for the courage to work through it together with him.

DAY 47: DESPAIR AND DEPRESSION

'When I try to change what I dislike in me by fighting it
I merely push it underground.
If I accept it, it will surface and evaporate.
What I resist, will stubbornly persist.' *(Anthony de Mello, S.J.*)*

Psalm 88

Are you surprised to find this psalm in the Bible? While most lament psalms turn to praise and thanksgiving towards the end, this one remains unrelievedly black.

Yet this is how life is for some people. The Israelites believed that even the worst experiences of life should be part of their worship.

At the bottom of the pit of despair the psalmist finds no meaning but keeps crying out to God in the hope that somewhere there will be a listening ear. This does not show lack of faith, but rather an enormous faith. It is much easier to believe in God when life trots along evenly, than when the rug is pulled out from under our feet.

Note that the person the writer blames is God's own self. There is the pain experienced in the breakdown of relationships (8,18), but the worst pain comes from the writer's feeling of abandonment by God. Verse 1 provides the only ray of hope: 'O Lord, the God who saves me' (NIV). God is called into the pit of despair with the sufferer, and if hope is distant, the only possibility of hope is that God will become present.

Dietrich Bonhoeffer wrote from prison before his death at the hands of the Nazis: 'The Bible directs us to the powerlessness and suffering of God; only a suffering God can help.' Read Matthew 27:45-56. Imagine yourself in that scene, knowing that Jesus died to enter completely into your situation with you.

** from **Wellsprings**, Gujarat Sahitya Prakash, Anand, 1990, reproduced by permission.*

DAY 48: IN FOR THE LONG HAUL

Read Hosea 11:1-9. What themes here would you pass on to someone you know is discouraged at the moment?

1 Peter 3:13 — 4:2, 12-19.

Discipleship is costly is the message behind much of this letter. Christians are encouraged to 'hang in' during the tough times.

The connection between 'discipleship' and 'discipline' is rarely highlighted when, glowing with hope and joy, we enter the Christian faith. For the Christians who originally received this letter, hope and joy had become muddied by the daily grind of life in a secular society.

To strengthen and encourage us on our Christian journey for when we face similar hard times, there are two important messages:

- No *real* harm will come to those who love God. This does not mean that Christians are excluded from suffering (at that time Christians were being martyred for their faith) but that nothing is able to break through the barrier of love and hope which God has given to the Christian.
- Suffering has meaning when it is a consequence of faith, because it joins us to God's *costly* struggle to bring the world to him.

This is not a cue for Christians to actively seek pain! Rather, it recognises that those who live according to God's values will tend to be at odds with the rest of the world. In some places, living according to God's values may lead to imprisonment or even death. However, living by God's values, even when such a life brings suffering, is ultimately a participation in God's loving, sacrificial work in and for the world.

Has your life become harder since you became a Christian? In what ways? Read 1 Peter 4:12-19 again, substituting your own name for the word 'friends'.

Checkpoint F

WHAT JESUS TEACHES ABOUT LIFE

INTRODUCTION TO READINGS 49–61

So far we have studied Biblical teaching about what it is to be human in a number of different ways:

- It means we are made in God's image, therefore to be part of the cosmic order of creation
- It is to be realistic about our mistakes, and our human need of God's continual re-creation and reconciling love
- God is interested and involved in every aspect of life, however insignificant it seems
- Human beings experience suffering, but also know that God wishes to be part of our painful experiences, as well as our joyful times.

Now, we turn to one of the most important aspects of human living: how we live and develop self-awareness in community — in love, friendship, family and wider social contexts.

Both the Song of Songs, which celebrates sexuality, and the Sermon on the Mount, which teaches about living responsibly, remind us that to be fully human is to recognise the connection between body and spirit. Acceptance of our bodies, with all their feelings attached, is as 'spiritual' as praying. Similarly, the wider 'body', or community, is a reflection of God's image when we recognise the love and respect God has for all people, and live accordingly.

DAY 49: LOVE TO RELY ON

Put on some music by a favourite female musician or singer that particularly inspires you. As you listen think of some of the 'strong' women you have known who have weathered many difficulties. What aspects of their character may have assisted them?

Ruth 1

In the world of Ruth and Naomi, the word for 'widow' meant 'silenced one'. A woman without a husband (or grown son) to care for her had no one to speak for her in society. She therefore had no position of importance within the family structure.

However, Ruth insists on having a voice. Moreover, she uses her voice to pledge her loyalty to another powerless, voiceless person. Because of Ruth's insistent loyalty and love, hope is born out of an otherwise hopeless situation. We note that the story starts with famine in Israel (2), and continues with 'famine' in their family as three of their men die (3-5). Naomi's return to her former home underlines how hopeless her situation is (20-21). Yet by the end of the story, not only is a harvest celebrated in the land, but Ruth has remarried and borne a son. Famine and hopelessness have given way to harvest and hope because two helpless women chose to exercise steadfast love towards each other.

'Steadfast love' (or 'kindness', in verse 8) is a term often used of God in the Bible. The story of Ruth shows that when human beings act with kindness and love, God is present in that action.

Jeremiah 31:3 reads: 'Israel, I will always love you; that's why I have been so patient and kind.' Imagine God saying this to you. What do you think this might mean for how you behave within your own family?

DAY 50: MAKING WISE CHOICES

'Your advice has been my guide,
and later you will welcome me in glory.
In heaven I have only you,
and on this earth you are all I want.' *(Psalm 73:24-25)*

Psalm 1

Our love and worship of God cannot be separated from listening to his teaching, a major theme of the Psalms (1,2). As we become familiar with God's law, we find much practical advice for life. Then, we have to put God's advice into practice 'day and night' (2), keeping it always in mind. Those choosing to live by God's advice produce 'fruit' and 'leaves' (3) in their lives which nurtures others. When we choose to make listening to God part of our lifestyle we will grow into a steadiness able to withstand hard times.

But if we choose to live without God, we are likely to be blown about by any wind sent by life (4). Then, because we have no grounding outside of ourselves, we cannot be connected to the source of life, nor find nourishment to help us grow into fruitfulness.

This psalm emphasises that our destiny is shaped by what we choose, a claim made of faith rather than experience. Other psalms reflect on why, despite choosing to live by God's advice, this does not automatically lead to an easy or 'successful' life. Blessing goes deeper than the obvious signs of 'success'. Luke's Gospel records Jesus' words: 'The people who are really blessed are the ones who hear and obey God's message!' (Luke 11:28)

Read Jesus' blessings, often called the Beatitudes (Matthew 5:3-12), an overture to the Sermon on the Mount (Matthew 5:3 — 7:29). Do you see yourself in any of these people?

DAY 51: SEXUAL DELIGHT

Reflect on your friendships and/or relationship. What areas of pain and frustration, joy and satisfaction are there?

Song of Songs 1:2-16

At some point in history, the Song of Songs was included in the Jewish Passover feast, to be read at the conclusion of the meal. Passover celebrates God's liberation of the Israelites from Egyptian slavery. The addition of the Song of Songs to the celebration is a powerful statement about the meaning of liberation. A glorious past historical event continues to be played out in the daily domestic lives of people, especially in the intimacy between persons. The Song emphasises the inward, intimate relationships and balances the external, historical celebration.

This reading introduces us to a book celebrating human sexuality. Its inclusion in the Bible makes us take seriously the close connection between sexuality and spirituality. Being able to accept and enjoy an intimate relationship with another person mirrors our ability to accept and enjoy an intimate relationship with God.

Western society tends to swing between extremes of puritanism and licentiousness in its attitudes towards sexuality. Both are far removed from what the Bible shows us to be God's intentions. The growing of whole, full relationships, including sexual pleasure and expression, is clearly part of being fully human.

The Song of Songs shows what was meant to be the outcome of Genesis 2: two people committed to a lifelong relationship, within which they are free to explore the heights of eroticism. The human body is celebrated for its beauty. To be human is to be spiritual *and* sexual.

*'I ask God for a special kind of body ... and get the one I have right now.' (Anthony de Mello, S.J., **Wellsprings**, Gujarat Sahitya Prakash, Anand, 1990, reproduced by permission.)*

What is your attitude to your body? Speak to God about your feelings.

DAY 52: LOVE'S JOY AND PAIN

Imagine you are in a quiet sunny spot. Now think back to a time when you fell in love. Feel the expectancy, the anguish, the embarrassment, the highs. Now reflect on and compare this experience to any present relationship. Allow yourself to share these reflections, positive or negative, with God.

Song of Songs 2:16 — 3:5

If the last reading celebrated the delights of intimacy, this reading expresses the difficulties. With any relationship, comes the possibility, even the probability, of pain.

From the cry of unity in love (16), the path of true love proves once again to be less than smooth. The restless longing and frustrated searching pictured in 3:1-3 mirrors the reality of any intimate relationship.

The richness of the Song of Songs lies in the way it merges the sexual with the spiritual. As with human relationships, so our relationship with God goes through periods of doubt and distance, where restless searching for longed-for intimacy can lead to periods of intense frustration. Anyone who has ever been in love knows exactly how this feels! In any relationship, human or divine, the loved one is intimately known, and at the same time remains a mystery.

Despite the possibility of pain, Song of Songs insists that love and intimacy are worth pursuing (2-3). A delicate balance can be found between knowing the loved one and accepting their mystery. The search for intimacy, whether with another person or with God, is part of growing and requires persistent effort.

Think about your relationship with God. Does God sometimes seem hard to find? Are there times when God might find you hard to pin down? Now think about the person or persons you feel most free to share your most intimate thoughts with and bring them before God.

DAY 53: LOVE'S DELIGHT AND MYSTERY

Play some favourite music, and while listening, imagine yourself enclosed in the circle of God's love.

Song of Songs 4:1-12

'Love changes everything', says a popular song. 'Love is blind' is a more cynical saying. This reading suggests that love is not blind; in fact, love sees more clearly what the beloved *can be*, and helps the beloved metamorphose, like a butterfly, into new possibilities.

The glory of love, as celebrated in this poem, is its ability to reflect glory onto the beloved. To be loved is to be seen as special, unique, wonderful. The intimate description of the lover in the poem lingers over and caresses every aspect of the beloved, delighting in sight, touch, sound, taste and scent. In such depths of intimacy, the human body becomes a sacrament, that is, a physical expression of something spiritual. It lies beyond the powers of description.

This metamorphosis into something special and beautiful is a feature of all love, both human and divine. To be loved by God is to be drawn into beauty, to become open to all sorts of possibilities within ourselves, ones not previously known. Each of us longs to feel special. Prayer, like love poetry, takes us into the realm of intimacy with the one who loves us and sees us as special. Being in love and being liberated by God changes everything. It changes how we see ourselves and others, how we see life, what meaning we find in living.

Reflect on opportunities that opened up for you because you felt secure in the love of God or another person.

DAY 54: GREAT MATES

'Love the Lord your God with all your heart, soul and mind. This is the first and most important commandment. The second most important commandment is like this one. And it is, "Love others as much as you love yourself."' (*Jesus, Matthew 22: 37-39*)

1 Samuel 18:1-5; 19:1-8

Jonathan fits the picture of the ideal friend. Imagine what it must have been like to be Jonathan, King Saul's son. Being the obvious successor to the throne of Israel, he learned all the princely things: how to lead the army, how to use with skill the various weapons, how to behave in court. As he grew up he became loved and admired by all the people in the land.

Then along comes David, a mere farm hand from the country. This insignificant lad kills the giant Goliath in true legendary style, and wins the admiration of all Israel. No one would have blamed Jonathan if he had grown jealous when a nobody usurped his position. But Jonathan loved David (3).

The depth of their friendship shows in the way in which Jonathan passed over to David all his personal signs of office. He handed over the royal robe and the military clothes and weapons that symbolised his position in court and army as the king's son. Jonathan's self-giving love saw David's potential. He saw that David, not himself, was the true successor to the throne because David was God's choice. Without Jonathan, David would probably not have survived Saul's murderous plots and become Israel's greatest king. Yet it is Jonathan the lesser known person, whose friendship makes the rest of the story possible.

How good a friend are you? Take some time to think about this, then ask God's help to continue learning how to be a friend.

DAY 55: 'ALL YOU NEED IS LOVE'

'God is the one who makes us patient and cheerful. I pray that he will help you live at peace with each other, as you follow Christ.' (Romans 15:5)

1 Corinthians 13

The letter of Paul's to the church at Corinth could be subtitled: 'All you need is love!'

It seems unbelievable that these people, shown unfailing love by God at all times, should fail to make love the basis of their life together. Yet this happened in the Corinthian church and often occurs today, well past the time of the Corinthian church.

Without love, all other accomplishments, no matter how admirable, become empty and meaningless, unable to give life to ourselves or to others.

Jesus quotes the Old Testament Scriptures, urging people to love God and each other (Matthew 22:37-39). Paul spells out exactly what it means to 'love'; it is difficult, and requires persistence and practice (4-7). His description ends in the difficult statement, 'Love never fails!' (8). We know that Paul is not thinking here of a nice, romantic 'they lived happily ever after' feeling, but rather of an attitude which comes about only through determination and will-power.

The final verses in this passage (11-13) put love in the context of growing into maturity. Working at love and persisting in relationships is part of our spiritual journey. Paul dares to state that love is even greater than faith and hope. Without it, the church cannot be a community that shows God's redeeming love to the world.

Read through verses 4-7 slowly. Make a list of what love is, and what love is not. Pin this list up in a place where you can see it regularly.

DAY 56: COUNT YOUR BLESSINGS

Do you know the old song 'Count your blessings, count them one by one'? Write down five good things about your everyday life now. Thank God for each of them, one by one.

Matthew 5:1-12

The blessings of Jesus are commonly known as the 'Beatitudes'. In modern times we might say 'Good on you!' to those who put these values into their daily lives.

Jesus uses the blessings to make the point that God prefers humans to live in a particular way so that we can fully enter into what he has provided for us. With each blessing, God not only congratulates those who have chosen this way, but also encourages others to change to this way.

The blessings set out in verses 3-11 picture life as it is meant to be, over against life as it usually is. Jesus is saying, in effect, 'This is what God meant when he created the world. This is how people were meant to live together.'

'...those who know they are spiritually poor' (3,GNB) realise that it is God who gives life and power. They are able to set out on life's journey. The lifestyle chosen then becomes one of renouncing the struggle to control and manipulate others. Rather, we will be drawn to other people, sharing their grief and showing mercy and peace.

Following God's way as set out by Jesus will be costly (11), but the reward is to experience life as God intended it to be.

Read the passage again. Underline the verse that speaks most clearly to you. Reflect quietly on this verse.

DAY 57: LIVING THE 10 COMMANDMENTS-1

Read the Ten Commandments (Deuteronomy 5:6-21).
Did any surprise you?

Matthew 5:21-32

The Ten Commandments set the outer limits for living in community under God. Outside the boundaries it was impossible for people to live together meaningfully.

Now Jesus fills in the boundary. The Ten Commandments were originally given as guidelines for God's people to flesh out, acting positively towards each other. But more and more these guidelines became hollow rules and regulations. As religion became legalistic its 'heart' went.

Jesus reminds the people that the original aim of the law was to give each person dignity and value. He insists that anger and scorn are as destructive as actual murder to another person (22). Destroying a person's self-esteem is like destroying their life. Also, God intended his people to live in a way that reflected his love and concern. Because of this, the worship of God becomes meaningless unless it goes hand-in-hand with care for others. There is no room for hypocrisy in this!

Similarly, the laws on marriage and divorce came to be applied oppressively to women. Jesus insists that women be treated as persons, not objects (28). He also refuses to see marriage as an ordinary contract that can be broken at the drop of a hat.

The main message in this passage is that human relationships are important. True community is built up by paying attention to relationships, inside and outside of the home. God is a God of relationships and community, so to worship God is to value relationships.

How do you normally view other people? Try seeing them through God's eyes, seeing each as a valuable person with an important place in the community.

DAY 58: LIVING THE 10 COMMANDMENTS - 2

In your relationships with family, friends and work colleagues, what do you find most difficult?

Matthew 5:33-48

The final verse in this passage sets our agenda for how we should live. It builds on what has come before: 'But you must always act like your Father in heaven.' (48)

What a hard task! Is Jesus simply setting up his followers for failure? Who can act like God? In reality Jesus is repeating a theme common in the Old Testament: we should choose to live in a particular way to reflect the character of God. If we have experienced God to be always loving and forgiving, a person who can be depended on to keep his promises and to deal with us more mercifully than we deserve, then this is how we also should be.

This is not a question of law but of loving response to the gracious action of God in the lives of his people.

Verse 43 is often taken to refer to an Old Testament teaching. This is a misreading of Jesus, who clearly places the saying in the mouths of 'people'. The consistent biblical teaching is to act with kindness and concern towards all people, including our enemies (see Proverbs 25:21), to reflect God's love and concern for them and to show a different way of living to that of taking revenge.

To act towards our opponents with love is to move out beyond our comfort zones, to treat with respect and act positively towards those with whom we feel uncomfortable. As Jesus points out, God does this all the time with us. Can we attempt less?

Think about the people who make you angry. Do you need to forgive them? Make a resolution to do something about it.

DAY 59: POSSESSIONS AND VALUES

'Your word is a lamp that gives light wherever I walk.
Your laws are fair, and I have given my word to respect them all.'
(Psalm 119:105-106)

Matthew 6:1-4, 19-21

Jesus' teachings on life are controlled by one consideration only: to show how life should be lived in the Kingdom of God. Under the rule of God, the world's values are turned upside down. Common attitudes and behaviour influenced by worldly considerations of power and control are shown to count for nothing in the Kingdom of God.

It was common practice at the time for good deeds to be done purely to earn social status, hence the warning not to show off when giving to charity (1-2). The Kingdom of God requires people to care for those less fortunate as an expression of God's love and concern for justice. No other reward, apart from that of spreading God's justice and love should be necessary.

Similarly, worldly values are turned upside down in the pursuit of security and possessions. Jesus shows that by placing too high a value on 'earthly treasures' (19) we become vulnerable, for they cannot provide more than a superficial, fragile security. To aim at gaining material wealth is to make way inevitably for greed, tyranny and social injustice.

To 'store up treasures in heaven' (20) does not mean we should become obsessed with securing a place in the afterlife. Rather, it means to invest in living the style of life demonstrated by Jesus: a life reflecting God's love and concern for all people, even at great cost to ourselves.

Take an inventory. What are your three most valued possessions? Are these 'on earth' or 'in heaven'? Ask God's help to invest in the values of the Kingdom.

DAY 60: NO WORRIES!

What is your main worry at the moment? Is it just a niggling worry or one that is crippling you? Tell God about it. Now spend time sitting quietly, concentrating on your breathing. As you breathe in slowly, feel peace flood into your body. As you breathe out, allow your worries and stress to flow out.

Matthew 6:25-34

It appears that obsessive worry about material security is not new! At the time when Jesus was speaking, the standard of living was nowhere near what many of us enjoy today. How much more do we need to hear these words!

The Kingdom of God is about liberation from anything which destroys life, and worry is a very destructive emotion. Chasing after more and more possessions is a subtle form of slavery, in which the chains can come in socially acceptable forms, such as mortgages, loan repayments and the like. Nonetheless, Jesus recognises that it is a slavery which prevents us from becoming totally free.

Jesus contrasts the anxiety-laden lifestyles of those caught up in materialism with the carefree lives of birds and flowers — living things which depend solely on God's provision for life. He is not suggesting that food and drink and clothing are unimportant. Rather, he asks us to get our priorities right — verse 33 encourages us to recognise that God's work of bringing in the Kingdom of God is the most important thing to think about.

Now think about what was worrying you earlier. Is it something really important or does it fit into the pattern of seeking material things? Whatever it is, share it with God. Allow him to help you carry your burden or change you attitude should that be necessary.

DAY 61: GETTING ALONG WITH OTHERS

'We know that God is always at work for the good of everyone who loves him. They are the ones God has chosen for his purpose.' *(Romans 8:28)*

Matthew 7:1-12

The teachings of Jesus are not for the faint-hearted. This passage presents a theme which runs throughout the Bible: our choices shape how we live our lives, and these choices matter!

Chapter 7, the final part of the collection of Jesus' teaching called 'The Sermon on the Mount', speaks about how we are to treat each other. The message comes through strongly that we are to be as sensitive to the needs and feelings of others as we would like others to be towards us. Verse 12 shows what an important theme this is. The Law (the Torah, the first five books of the Bible) and the Prophets (most of the rest of the Hebrew Bible) devote time to teaching us to recognise the value of each person, to make sure that everyone in society has their rights respected.

An important aspect of community living is to be willing to look critically at ourselves from time to time (3-5). Healthy living involves growing self-awareness, as well as growing intimacy with others. Without humble self-assessment, we too easily fall into the trap of criticising others.

To be Christian is to follow the way of Jesus in daily discipleship. Although this is not an easy way to live (14), help is always at hand. Verses 7-11 stress God's willingness to give to those who truly seek his assistance. If we, imperfect as we are, can still be loving, nurturing parents, imagine how much more our heavenly Parent wants to give to us.

Have your relationships with family and friends changed at all since becoming a Christian? Do they need to change?

USING FOOTHOLD IN A GROUP

As you read *Foothold: Knowing Ourselves* things you already know about being human will be confirmed for you. But other topics will affect you personally and deeply as the word of God challenges and confronts you. To get the most from these studies, you and members of your group will need to learn to share ideas and feelings at a closer level than what some may be used to. Members will need to maintain trust and confidentiality. Not all issues will be clear-cut and at times you may need to agree to disagree. The Bible text is sometimes silent when we seek explicit guidance (see ‘Knowing what God wants us to do’, p. 28).

It is good to meet regularly, keeping in step with everyone’s personal reading pattern. At the beginning, decide how often you will meet and for how long. A new group should probably aim at sessions of one and a half or two hours. Eight or ten sessions would be a good target.

Scripture Union has developed a simple method for personal Bible reading. You will find this on page 2. We have adapted this for use in the group sessions (see below).

If possible, rotate leaders. This spreads the discussion and develops people’s gifts. Allow space for the shy and less articulate to put their views, and encourage members to keep to the topic of the day. Keep a list of additional questions that crop up and discuss these at the end of each session or in a separate session at the end of the series.

To break the ice, start meetings with simple refreshments. This helps those new to group Bible study or who don’t know each other well to relax, and also accommodates late arrivals. Allow about 10 minutes for this.

Begin with brief introductions. Arrange beforehand who will open and close the session. It is not fair to ask new members to do this before they are at ease with the group. Some may never feel comfortable in this task.

Use an up-to-date version of the Bible such as the *Contemporary English Version.* Encourage members to look at the scripture passage afresh, before putting forward simple queries. Give your group the choice of focusing on the passages they have been reading alone or using the passages listed below.

SECTION	**THEME**	**BIBLE PASSAGES**
A	Our image and responsibilities	Genesis 1:26-28; 3:1-13.
B	God's connection with us	Romans 7:9-25
C	Full humanity	Philippians 2:1-11
D	God's concern for the whole of life	1 Timothy 4:1-10
E	Living with suffering	Job 10:1-15
F	Love & friendship	Ruth 1
G	Practical Christian living	Matthew 6:1-4, 19-21
H	Resurrection lifestyle	Colossians 3:1-17
I	Wise living	Proverbs 13:1 — 14:8
J	Living in the light of the future	Romans 8:12-27

The Checkpoints at the beginning of each *Foothold* section will have opened up the broad issues of the topic so you can now start discussing any challenging issues that have arisen for group members or work through the selected passages above. Either way, the following questions will get discussion started:

- What is the passage about? (Try writing a 6 word headline.)
- Is there something here that confirms your own thinking about being human?
- What specially strikes you in this passage? Is there anything new to you? Or maybe, something to re-think?
- Is there anything to note for personal review later — perhaps something you are not quite ready for yet? (You may not want to share this with the group at this stage.)
- What other questions do you want to list for later discussion?
- How might the study change — or encourage — your living?

Finish discussion on time.

Have the leader bring together some of the matters discussed. Then take them up in simple sentence prayers, bringing any other requests for prayer before God.

PLANNING FOR NEXT SESSION

Make arrangements now for the next meeting. What worked and what didn't? What changes to the format are required? Where will you meet? When? Who will pray, lead, provide refreshments?

Checkpoint G

PRACTICAL CHRISTIAN LIVING

INTRODUCTION TO READINGS 62–74

Community living, as God sees it, is based on covenant — mutual commitments based on promises. This goes for relationships between ourselves and God, but also between people. The state of living in a community that is harmonious in all aspects has a special Hebrew word: *shalom*. This signifies wholeness and peace between people, God and all of creation.

These next readings emphasise the importance of justice for *shalom*. It is amazing how much of the Bible is concerned with teachings on justice, especially the importance of caring for those without the means of caring for themselves (foreigners, widows, orphans, etc).

Many of the passages setting out God's Law in the Hebrew Bible stress responsibility to these people. However, it is not simply seen as a legal obligation. Leviticus and Deuteronomy constantly mention that God has saved Israel from an oppressive regime (Egypt), so they must not live in any way that oppresses others. Leviticus 19 repeats the phrase 'I am the Lord your God' as reason for obedience to the Law. In other words, because God is God, and interest in justice is basic to the character of God, the Law is basic to the character of humanity as well as being a reflection of God.

It is important continually to ask ourselves who the landless, strangers, unemployed and unprotected people are in our society. The New Testament also shows us that concern for justice is a matter always under consideration for God's people. Justice belongs not only in societal structures, but also in personal relationships. *Shalom* is threatened by guilt and lack of forgiveness, as well as by imbalance of wealth between the rich and poor. Restoring *shalom* may be difficult, even sacrificial, as the story of Zacchaeus tells us, but is necessary for life if it is to be lived as God desires.

DAY 62: JUSTICE MEANS FREEDOM

Justice for the poor, the foreigner and the disadvantaged is clearly God's intention. Racism, broken relationships and injustice are not. Freedom of spirit is, but this depends on how far we practise justice.

Leviticus 19:9-18

Selfish attitudes can deny the generous spirit encouraged in this passage (9,10). God's guidelines consistently benefit both the receiver and the doer. The poor and foreigners (10) receive what they need from the excess of the harvest, while doing God's will blesses the harvester.

The modern track record on justice is not good. In the materialistic West, unequal distribution of resources continues to grow. Unfairness flourishes. Governments budget large amounts of money for tanks or warplanes, money that could be used to wipe out disease in countless villages. This is not in keeping with the 'golden rule' (18) and is equivalent to stealing and cheating (11,13).

Compassion is an integral part of justice. Is it a coincidence that Christian missions were often the first to care for, rather than profit from, inhabitants of the so-called 'third world'? Or that the first organisations to focus on the deaf and blind (14) were Christian societies who saw the image of God in the lives of these people considered to be valueless?

Closer to home, we too need to follow these principles. Genuine charity has distinct benefits, both for giver and receiver. 'Keeping the rage' (18) or seeking revenge extracts a price in bitterness, even stomach ulcers and ruined relationships! A better alternative is not to hold grudges (17), freeing us to forgive, to love, and to be loved.

1. Examine an important political issue this week by reading newspapers and watching TV from God's vantage point.
2. Treat everyone you meet today with the dignity of a person created in the image of God deserves. Don't stop today!

DAY 63: RULES FOR RIGHT RELATIONSHIPS

Third world debt has led some Christians to suggest a Jubilee-type* new beginning. This would enable poor countries to escape from their debt trap. Some criticise banks for their ever-increasing charges and massive profits. Does the Bible have principles that apply to such situations?

Deuteronomy 24:10-22

Mark Twain is supposed to have said: 'It's not the things in the Bible I don't understand that trouble me; it's the things in the Bible I *do* understand'! Today's passage could be one of these. Using examples of loans, especially to the poor (12), fair pay for work (15), individual responsibility for crime (16) and treatment of the powerless (17), Moses could well be commenting on some of today's ills.

Some commentators believe that the Bible shows God has a bias towards the poor. One response is that God is fair, and shows favour to no-one. A passage like this, however, shows without doubt that God's heart is with the poor, the dispossessed and the powerless. So, those who claim to follow God, have a duty to care for them too (18,22).

Whether we are capitalists (10), employers (14), members of a dysfunctional family (16), borrowers (12), orphans, widows or foreigners (19), God has a word for us all. The word is that we are responsible for each other, especially those in need, and also responsible for our own actions. If we follow these guidelines God will notice (13), but if we do not, there will be consequences (15). Sadly, we reap the harvest of disobedience in the breakdown of so much of our society today — with homelessness, poverty, violence, and abuse of all kinds.

Compared with the majority of the world, most of us are rich. How can we respond practically to the principles of verses 19-22?

* *Every fiftieth year in Israel, all slaves were to be liberated, ancestral possessions restored, the land rested and kept fallow (Leviticus 25).*

DAY 64: FIRST THINGS FIRST

You may feel possessive or proud about your looks, possessions, physical prowess, parents, but can you claim responsibility for them? Reflect on, 'All things come from you, O Lord, and of your own have we given you', a once familiar thanksgiving used in church after the offering was received.

Deuteronomy 26:1-11

Old-fashioned church harvest festivals where children bring pumpkins or cans of baked beans for the local nursing home may sometimes seem inappropriate in today's cities. Yet the principles of giving God the first part of the harvest (2) are still relevant, despite the global drift to the cities where harvest time is unknown.

Tithing (giving God the first tenth of what we receive, 12) is to be done in thankfulness and worship (2-4) not through duty or fear. The people of Israel look back to their recent past in Egypt, remembering the bad times (6). Rescued, they are to be blessed with abundance (1,9). Overflowing with gratitude, they are asked to give their first and best to share with others, partying with God (2,3).

This may sound odd to those caught up in 'economic rationalism'. Today, many farmers are required to 'set aside' land, paid *not* to grow crops. This is an obscenity with so much starvation in a world of plenty. Where profit and the 'bottom line' dominates economics and politics, the church is called to lead and be different. In doing so, we rediscover God's paradox — the more we give, the more we receive. When governments cut overseas aid, are they in danger of depriving themselves of God's blessing? An interesting thought. Then, how about us?

Does verse 11 have anything to say to your situation, about hospitality, about Christian celebration, and about church community life? What one practical step can you take to respond to this?

DAY 65: CURING INSOMNIA

Name the things that trouble you and keep you awake. Bring them to God.

Psalm 32

Guilt feelings are unhealthy, psychologists tell us, with some implying they should not be addressed. The psalmist sees guilt is a fact and has unhealthy side-effects (3,4). If we face the problem and deal with it, we experience the freedom of sin forgiven. Forgiveness brings freedom to both forgiver and forgiven. To harbour resentfulness and retain a bitter, unforgiving spirit is a pernicious poison. But God is not like this and longs for all to be freed from the effects of sin (1). The way towards blessing is to acknowledge our sin, bring it into the open, and allow God to deal with it (2).

Covering up the causes of our sin takes time and energy. Pretending they don't exist, sweeping or rationalising them away is no help, nor is shifting the blame, saying 'It's not my fault'. To ignore them can be costly, resulting in psychosomatic illnesses related to suppressed emotions. We need transparent openness and honesty with God, who knows all about us anyway, with each other, and most of all, with ourselves!

The pay-off for confession and genuine repentance is a lightness of spirit (7), cause for celebration (11). God takes the initiative: 'You protect' … 'you put songs in my heart' … 'you have saved' … (7) and 'you said'… (8). We do not deserve this. God's grace provides it, promising guidance and freedom to boot — we don't have to be reined in like horses and mules (8,9). Perhaps the best antidote for insomnia is a clear conscience!

Search your mind for any unconfessed sin. What can you do about unhealthy guilt — a telephone call, a postcard, a letter? Or should you make an appointment to see someone? Do it!

DAY 66: WHAT DOES GOD'S PROTECTION MEAN?

I have hard questions as I read this psalm. A missionary friend spent 37 years establishing a church in a very difficult situation. Soon after retirement she was diagnosed with terminal cancer, and died; a colleague was killed in a hijacked plane crash; another's legs were amputated after a terrorist bomb attack in Zaire; thousands of Christians in Rwanda lost loved ones in the genocide there; and I have buried many babies and children. What hard questions do you want to ask God?

Psalm 91

Jesus quoted part of this psalm (11,12) when tempted by the devil (Luke 4:10,11). That should squash superficial beliefs that being a disciple brings an easy life. Experience tells us this is not so. Jesus invites us not only to follow him, but to take up our cross every day! (Luke 9:23) Some Christians teach that prosperity is proof we are living God's way. But when suffering comes, as it surely will at some stage, we find this teaching to be deceptive. Ultimately such teaching is heresy: it contradicts Christian faith and truth.

Many find life does not turn out as the psalmist describes (7-10). Is he whistling in the wind? Paul has the same assurance even in the face of unbelievable hardships. Nothing can separate him from the love and protection of God (Romans 8:35). God's ways are not our ways, but both David and Paul (2) have a basic trust that God can carry us through any trap or disease (3), dangers or disasters (5,6). It is a painful journey, but as the Book of Job shows, God is there, waiting for our call, waiting to answer, to protect us and honour our trust (15).

Where was God in your hardest times? And now?

DAY 67: A COSTLY COMMODITY

Think of times in your life when you have been forgiven and times when you have found it too hard to forgive. Open up to God your positive and negative experiences.

Luke 19:1-10

There are many ways through repentance and confession to forgiveness. For Zacchaeus, curiosity was the first step. Judging by his undignified action(4), he must have been *very* curious! Their encounter is revealing (5). Jesus took the initiative, reaching out with warmth, not judgment and Zacchaeus instantly responded with enthusiasm. Everyone else (7) reacted differently which is understandable, for Zaccheus had probably been 'ripping them off' for years! It would be fascinating to have observed what Zacchaeus did between meeting Jesus that day and his public promise to make restitution later.

Many people come to faith after little or no previous contact with the church. Later, they often tell a similar tale, how they felt accepted by their fellow Christians who tactfully refrained from commenting on aspects of their life style. Continuing with their normal patterns of living, they come to realise strongly that they must discontinue certain habits or practices. They can only explain this feeling as the work of the Holy Spirit urging them to bring their new life into line with God's way.

This seems to have happened to Zaccheus. His offer to give back four times what he had taken was actually only the legal minimum. It was not the act of restitution that saved him (9) — Ephesians 2:8,9 makes that clear — but it was a good indication he had already started a new life. The 'punch-line'(10) gives hope to all, however lost they might seem.

Do you feel the need to make restitution to someone — to whom, and for what? Why not begin now?

DAY 68: HALLELUJAH, ANYWAY!

Who is truly content among those you know? What makes them so? What stops you?

1 Timothy 6:6-10,17-19

Wealth is not a sin but how we use our wealth matters. What we give to God does not measure our spirituality, rather what we keep for ourselves. I have had reason to visit desperately poor countries. I can't help but notice the joy radiating from many of the people. Despite hardship their generosity to visitors is abundant. In contrast, some of the world's most miserable people are those with the most possessions. Jesus taught about money, camels, and the eye of a needle (Mark 10:23-5). And Paul pursues the theme with young Timothy, warning him of the dangers associated with wealth — the temptations and traps (9), the destruction that goes with unsatisfied greed (9,10), even the loss of faith (10).

We tend to idolise self-made millionaires, who think not in thousands but in billions of dollars. They could not spend all their money if they tried. Some have found themselves in jail because of how they made their money. Others are being pursued through the courts.

How illogical to idolise the wealthy. We can't take our wealth with us (7). It is easily lost (17) as those who have suffered losses through the stock market and property speculation know.

Wealth should be shared. Those funding projects that bear fruit for the Gospel or enable needy people to become independent find true joy. To give wealth away to a worthy cause is more satisfying than the loneliness of people such as the former President Mobutu, whose greed destroyed Zaire. For those of us less rich, we should be content that our basic needs are satisfied, and recognise that true wealth comes from faith in God.

What things that you rarely use could you do without? Think of good ways of disposing of them.

DAY 69: PREFERENTIAL TREATMENT

Do you have a secret yearning? Designer clothes, overseas travel, expensive model cars, a luxury home? If you could satisfy this, would it change or improve your life? In what ways?

James 2:1-7; 5:1-6

James gives a terrifying warning to rich people (5:1-6). But he also scolds those who treat the rich preferentially and put down the poor. If we are honest, we are all guilty of this to some degree. In our churches, pastors can be tempted not to take issue with wealthy or influential members in case they withdraw their support. And in missionary or charitable organisations that depend on the donations of supporters, there is always the danger that large donors will be treated differently from those sending the 'widow's mite'.

The exploitation of the poor is a common biblical theme and is again mentioned here (5:4). God loathes any exploitation. Today exploitation has become a sin with global as well as individual dimensions. The gap between rich and poor is growing and concerned Christians are campaigning for ways to cancel the debts crippling the capacity of poorer countries to survive. One suggestion is something along the lines of the Old Testament Jubilee (Leviticus 25).

As always, God will have the last say. James tells us we can best learn about faith by turning to the poor (2:5). Those who have been to the developing world know all too well how often the faith of Christians there puts us in the wealthy West to shame.

Think back to times where you have looked after the concerns of the rich or privileged rather than the disadvantaged. Think of opportunities you might find to begin to reverse the trend this coming week!

DAY 70: TENANT PROBLEMS

It is not easy for a landlord to remove unruly tenants even when they damage property. It is even more difficult to remove our most troublesome tenant — the tongue. When did you last wish you had put your brain into gear before opening your mouth and allowing your tongue to cause unnecessary damage?

James 3:1-18

James suggests that a test of maturity is whether we can control our tongue. If we can do that, we can manage the rest of our body. We all have examples where either our tongue or another's has hurt and damaged someone. Again, James does not mince words (6,8). He identifies the source of our verbal lack of control — the 'evil power', who wants to see Jesus' disciples lose control. The tongue lets loose its deadly poison in Christian circles just as much as in secular ones. Church synods and assemblies, as well as church newspapers and various gossip grapevines provide plenty of evidence of this.

But it does not have to be so, nor should it be! The tongue can also be the source of much blessing — to encourage, share the good news, forgive, apologise, teach the truth, praise God, pray for others. It should reflect all the virtues of verses 17 & 18. Marlene Cohen recently wrote a book called *The Divided Self**. There she focuses on the precise point James is making: we need to seriously question the genuineness of the good that comes via our tongues if evil comes too (14-16). The answer to James' questions in verses 11 & 12 is clearly, 'No!'

'...plant seeds of peace, they will harvest justice' (18). What can you initiate today that will make good use of your tongue in the way God intended?

** Marshall Pickering, an imprint of Harper Collins, London, 1996.*

DAY 71: LOVE-HATE RELATIONSHIPS

'I love people... It's *particular* people I can't stand!'
Think about the thin line between love and hate in your close relationships.

1 John 3:1-3, 11-18

Father love has received a bad press in our generation, sometimes deservedly so. On more than one occasion I have heard a person say in anguish, 'If God is meant to be our Father, I don't want anything to do with him'. For these people, their human fathers were off-course, failing to imitate the divine model by such a long way. God wants us to experience a real parent-child relationship and the ultimate sign of that love is finding it can be trusted. God does provide for all our needs both physical and emotional, and can always be depended on. And even that assurance is only a pale shadow of what is yet to come (2). As we experience God's love we should be motivated to imitate Jesus, God's son, in every aspect of our living. It should come as a response to his love (3), not from fear of punishment.

Godlessness, murder, envy, evil (12), and hatred (15) are the antithesis of what God intends for our relationships. But as we observe those close to us and gorge on what we are fed daily in the media, we quickly see these characteristics dominate our world. Leading such a lifestyle brings about extreme and permanent consequences (15). The alternate lifestyle to which Jesus calls his followers demands that we love one another. It is plain, straightforward love achieved by helping others (18), by caring for those in need (17) especially believers, and by self-sacrifice, our supreme model being Jesus himself (16).

How can you best respond to verses 17 and 18?

DAY 72: LOVE BEYOND MEASURE

'Jesus, do you love me?', a girl asked. 'You know I do.' 'How much do you love me, Jesus?' she asked. 'I can't love you any more than I do right now'. 'Yes, but how *much* do you love me?' she asked again. Stretching his arms as wide as they could go, he replied: 'I love you *this* much!' — and they nailed him to the cross.

1 John 4:7-21

Love is costly, very different from the idealised love of novels and glossy magazines. For some it only lasts while the 'feel-good' factor is there, leaving to start again when it's gone. Our throwaway society encourages a pale reflection of the real thing. Real love (10) is not concerned with feeling good *about* someone else, even God. Real love is modelled on Jesus' costly love who forfeited his life so we could live. As disciples, living will prove costly for us also.

The litmus test of love is clear-cut — that we love one another (7,11). God took the initiative in loving us (9,10,14 and especially 19), giving us all the resources we need to live as he intended. God's Spirit (13) bears fruit in us (Galatians 5:22,23) making love for others possible. Love is the first fruit of the Spirit. See Paul's checklist in 1 Corinthians 13 and ponder how practical it is!

Fear of divine punishment shows we have yet to learn what real love is. The antidote to that fear, and the worry that goes with it, is equally straightforward — love others, and live as Christ did (17). The responsibility is ours.

What fruits of the Spirit in Galatians 5 are your strong points? What do you lack (see 1 Corinthians 13)? Thank God for your strong points and ask God to work with you on what you lack.

DAY 73: RENOVATE YOUR LIFE

What things from your past always bring feelings of regret or guilt? Quietly tell God about them.

Romans 8:1-11

In chapter 7 Paul shares his struggles to deal with the opposing forces at work within him. We too share his natural tendency towards sin, for our behaviour is often contrary to our maker's design (7:25). But we have access to a divine resource, the Holy Spirit, who makes the alternative way viable, creating for us a life of freedom rather than imprisonment (2); of spirituality rather than selfish appetites (5); of peace (6) rather than a fear of death.

Recently I received a letter from Rwanda. Though well past, the consequences of the horrific genocide of 1994 linger on, and will continue for a long time. Over 80,000 people are in prison, charged with complicity in the mass murders. Fear and suspicion is still rife. A pastor I know well has been imprisoned because of the false allegations of three people with a grudge against him. His case may take decades to come to court because the system cannot cope.

Priorities are quickly focused for people like my pastor friend. He may be imprisoned unjustly and may actually die there, but his spirit is free. Death and fear don't inhibit him. He is able to express his faith effectively, with joy. In two months recently, 50 new believers were baptised as a result of his ministry and the work of the Holy Spirit. He is a living example of verse 10. Although he may not avoid the punishment of the state, he is assured of the same resurrection as Jesus, 2000 years ago!

How can you be sure verse 11 is true? Will you allow it to make a difference in your life, today?

DAY 74: FIGHT THE GOOD FIGHT

Can you recall one or two recent examples on TV, at the movies or in your local shopping centre, where you have either seen examples of God's Spirit or of people tempted by selfish desires?

Galatians 5:16-26

If our selfish desires are in control we are not being guided by or controlled by the Spirit of God (16). We all make excuses, saying 'I can't help myself', 'It's not my fault'. We may be wanting revenge, watching our weight go up and doing nothing about it, or constantly giving into our weaknesses. These (19) are contrary to God's intentions for us. Paul does not mince his words, and paints a vivid, realistic and troubling picture of his world and ours. It is not the temptations that are wrong, but what we do about them.

'Temptations ... are useful because they can make us humble, they can cleanse us, and they can teach us. All of the saints passed through times of temptation and tribulation, and they used them to make progress in the spiritual life. Those who did not deal with temptations successfully, fell to the wayside', wrote 14th century mystic, Thomas à Kempis, who saw great value in the battle.

Temptations affect our religious worldview (20), relationships (20), behaviour (19,21), thought patterns and attitudes (19,20). It makes no sense to choose such ways, for we suffer most when we give in. The alternatives are striking (22,23): liberating and life-changing for us and for others. How different the world would be if people consistently lived out these characteristics. Paul says that no-one can stop us living that way, if we choose to do so (23b). It is one of the ultimate benefits of exercising the freedom of will which is God's gift to all who trust in Christ.

If 'temptations reveal who we are', as Thomas à Kempis writes, who are you?

LIVING THE RESURRECTION LIFESTYLE

INTRODUCTION TO READINGS 75–80

'Resurrection' means a life that bursts through the dimensions of space and time in God's invisible, imperishable, incomprehensible domain. This is what is meant by 'heaven' — not the heaven of the astronauts, but God's heaven. It means going into reality, not going out.

(Hans Küng, ***Does God Exist?*** *Collins/Doubleday, 1978)*

Paul founded the church in Corinth, but never visited Colossae. However, he felt a strong responsibility to encourage and nurture both, especially to impress on the Christians that they were now living *post-resurrection*. In other words, his message to them (and to us) is to live now in the light of Christ's *future!*

The letters spell out what 'eternal life' is: a quality, rather than a quantity. To live in the light of Christ's resurrection now must have consequences for all areas of human life, and these following readings explore some of these areas. Marriage relationships, personal purity, vocation, rights and responsibility are all to come under the light of new life in Christ. To live as if unaware of the resurrection is to live as if 'our message is worthless', and faith is meaningless.

Perhaps the most challenging aspect of Paul's teaching in these readings is that of human mortality. How is mortality to be understood post-resurrection? Paul acknowledges mortality as being part of the order of creation, but stresses that Christians should live in constant expectation of the return of Christ. For Paul, this return was expected imminently, so people were urged to live literally as if each day was their last. It is hard to sustain this sense of urgency, two thousand years down the track, but it still presents an important challenge to us to re-evaluate our lifestyle. We need to question whether this has an 'eternal' quality about it and if not, begin, with God's help to make the necessary changes.

The right gear

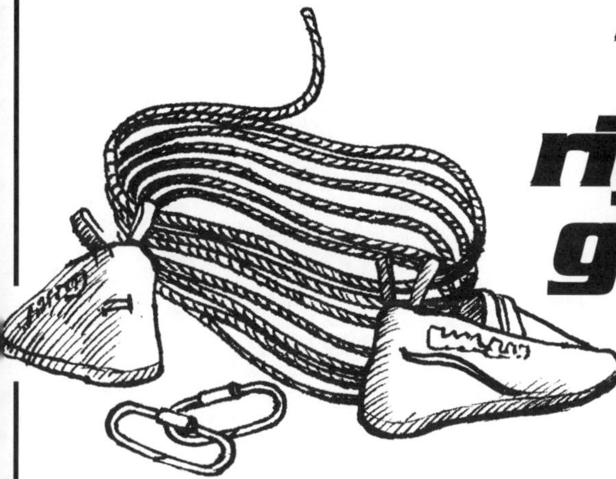

With the help of Foothold you have begun your adventure with the Bible... and with God.

Now let Scripture Union's other resources help you to keep going.

Scripture Union has for over 100 years been providing meditation resources to help people grow with the Bible.

On many occasions in the Bible, God's word is described as bread, milk, meat - food for the Christian's journey through life.

After you have completed this book in the *Foothold* series, take some decisions to firm up your faith. Equip yourself on a regular basis for faithful Christian living. Aim to find day-by-day nourishment for your life.

Order the other two books in the *Foothold* series or check out the quarterly Bible guides published by Scripture Union. They're available for you and for people of all ages (including children and young people). They're for people new to regular Bible reading and experienced Christians alike.

Use the coupon below to put yourself in touch with these resources. There are more details on the next page. Cut out the coupon and send it to your nearest Scripture Union office.

The address is on page 126.

Dear Scripture Union,

I am interested to know more about Scripture Union's Bible resources. Please supply the information as indicated on the reverse of this reply coupon.

My name ______________________

Address ______________________

____

Postcode ______________________

Scripture Union's Bible resources... for a firm foothold on faith

Foothold
The other two books in the series will give you a firmer grip on the Bible's message and help you find a *Foothold* for your faith. Each book has another 100 specially selected Bible readings. *Understanding the Bible* will give you a quick overview of what the Bible is really about. You will explore the central message of the most popular book of all time. The stories and themes will begin to hang together and you will feel more confident about your faith. *Knowing Ourselves* will give you insights about how God sees the great variety of human beings he created. We discover his dreams for people alongside their stumbles and failings. We begin to see ourselves - our strengths and weaknesses through the eyes of the characters and teachings of the Bible. A different perspective altogether!

Daily Bread
Scripture Union's best seller! A quarterly book for adults with devotional readings for every day. The comments from an international team of writers are direct, practical and zesty. Also available in large print format. Includes outlines for group discussion and a variety of features.

Encounter with God
A thought provoking Bible reading quarterly for people who like to be stretched. Ideal for experienced Bible readers.

Closer to God
These Bible readings are for anyone who believes or hopes that God speaks to ordinary people: loving, freeing, changing and healing them in today's world.

Something for everyone
There are Scripture Union resources for all age groups from pre-schoolers to adults.

Dear Scripture Union,
Please send

❑ a sample copy of Daily Bread and a full catalogue of Scripture Union Bible resources.
❑ information about becoming a local church representative to promote Bible reading in my congregation.

Remember to print you name and address on the front of this reply coupon and send to your nearest office of Scripture Union. The address is on page 126 of this book.

DAY 75: WHAT I THINK IS WHAT I AM

'You are what you eat' is a well known saying. What does it say to you?

Colossians 3:1-17

Who we are affects what we think, says Paul. And what we are is the focus needed (1). Our status as believers is determined by what Christ has done for us (Romans 5:8). A friend became a Christian during a church service in Wales. Immediately after, he was given a long list of Christian 'don'ts' which included dancing, cinema, smoking, swearing and being within a certain distance of a member of the opposite sex — enough to put anyone off the journey before it was even started! But Paul says that although keeping rules gives the appearance of godliness, this won't help us overcome desires that control us (2:20-23). In today's passage, Paul lists at least fourteen negative commands (5-9) and twelve positive ones (12-17). Is he contradicting himself? Not at all.

The commands here reflect a Christlike lifestyle, different in kind to negative rules (2:21). Knowing that our thoughts affect our behavior, our motivation should not come from a teeth-clenching sense of Christian duty, but in response to how Christ has treated us and chosen us (12). How then can we change our thought patterns so that our Christian communities conform to Christ's pattern? By allowing Christ to give us peace between people, peace in the fellowship (15), which in turn will control our actions and thoughts. Cause and effect. His is the initiative, the response is ours.

How comfortable are you with Jesus as your companion today, knowing he is aware of all you think and say and do? Consciously discuss matters with him as you go about your work and leisure.

DAY 76: LOVE, SEX, MARRIAGE AND DIVORCE

When couples enter marriage, divorce is not dreamed to be possible. Finding proof texts from the Bible is no great source of comfort when things sour. The grace of God is. Bring your relationship, positive or flawed, before God.

1 Corinthians 6:15 — 7:16

Paul apparently felt no need for the companionship of a partner (8), but he understood that not all were like him (7). What he also understood was the potential human weakness that can damage all of us 'in a way that no other sin' can (18). Church assemblies and leaders seem unsure of the rights and wrongs of issues of sexuality and divorce. They swing between harsh judgmentalism and merciless legalism to a liberal toleration of an 'anything-goes-so-long-as-there-is-love' mentality. Paul is seen by many as a narrowminded, intolerant, conservative killjoy. But his advice (18) is clear and godly: 'don't be immoral in matters of sex'. If we are, there is a costly price to pay.

As to marriage, sex and divorce, unpopular as some of his language may be in today's society, the biblical principles are clear and unquestionable — marriage is for mutual comfort (7:2), an exercise in mutual self-giving (3-6), and celibacy is a positive option (7,8). Divorce is not God's ideal, but under certain conditions (15) is permissible. Subsequent marriage is an issue for many churches. The influence of a believing spouse has eternal consequences for the whole family (14). With family breakdown escalating (as never before), even in Christian families, we need more than ever the resources of the Holy Spirit to survive — whether it be within the tensions of difficult marriages, the strains of the generation gap between parents and children, or the pressures of celibate loneliness. Thank God, those resources are freely available. We only need to ask!

How can you treat your 'temple of the Holy Spirit' (6:19) better today?

DAY 77: LIVE RIGHT AND LOVE THE LORD

If you had only a short time to live, how would you re-arrange your priorities?

1 Corinthians 7:17-40

Today, when most people expect to have multiple jobs in their working life, if fortunate enough to have them, Paul's opening advice (17,21,22) is less relevant to us than to his readers. A recent church survey showed a substantial number of church attenders have changed churches in recent years. Loyalty to the local congregation seems to be fading. Paul's advice about not changing our religious status (18,19) therefore may be less appropriate today than it was then. He was convinced that the Lord would be returning soon. For their own good, Paul advised the Corinthian believers not to be sidetracked from the job of preparing for that great day. This warning is still appropriate for us, but perhaps not all of the specific advice.

The fundamental principle remains unchanged for us: in our lifestyle and vocation we should live out our priorities, believing the Lord will come again soon, like 'a thief in the night'. What matters most to us — our job, our marriage, or daily life? Is it an end in itself, or the means to serving God with all our heart, soul, mind and strength? For many, sadly, the daily treadmill of life becomes a boring routine. Whether we are married or not (27,29), whether we are going through good times or bad, whether we are rich or poor (30), all will pale into insignificance in eternity (31). Paul is a realist. He knows marriage has its problems (33,34) and suggests celibacy may be a preferable option (40).

What should you be doing to be ready for Jesus? 'Just do it!' as a famous sportswear advertisement puts it.

DAY 78: MUZZLING THE BULLOCK

'I don't agree with what you say, but I would give my life for your right to say it', Voltaire is reputed to have said during turbulent times in France. Paul, an unlikely soul mate, asserted his rights as a follower of Jesus, but chose to abdicate those rights. Give thanks for faithful volunteers you know who have forgone their rights to salaries, not unlike Paul the tentmaker.

1 Corinthians 9:1-18

Not everyone was convinced that Paul was an apostle as he was not one of the twelve chosen by Jesus. But the Corinthians were in no doubt — they were living proof he was. Others questioned Paul's rights (4,5,11,12). With so many rights movements worldwide — women's, gay, animal, minority — what Paul says is very much to the point. He gives an extended run-down on the whole question of 'rights' (1-12), using the word no fewer than 6 times. But in dealing with the criticism he faces, he makes a revealing shift from 'rights' to 'privileges' (15,18). Rights are a privilege, and privilege demands responsibility. Those demanding rights today should ensure they have a corresponding regard for their responsibilities.

Paul draws our attention to the particular right of the gospel worker to receive material support. Using the analogy of a bullock (9), he implies that the preacher (17) has the right to be paid for this privileged occupation. There is a dual responsibility here: the preacher/pastor/ missionary must earn the right to be paid for his/her hard work, while supporters should be generous, not 'muzzling the bullock' (9). Wouldn't it be good if churches and charities could concentrate on their job without constantly pleading for funds! A more generous spirit would achieve that aim.

What rights do you see as important for yourself? For members of your family? Church? Community? For everyone?

DAY 79: THE LAST ENEMY

After suffering a series of small strokes, my elderly mother is in a nursing home gradually winding down. It is sad to see how much vivacity and energy she has lost. She is lovingly cared for with others also on the last leg of their journey. We cannot escape our mortality. Reflect on your diminishing senses or another's.

1 Corinthians 15:12-28

The central fact for Christians is that Christ was raised from death (12). Ocassionally a church leader publicly says that they don't believe in his resurrection. Paul says bluntly that if we don't believe in this, 'our message is worthless, and so is your faith' (14) which is then useless (17). If physical death is the end of the story, despair will gradually cripple us.

Coming back from the nursing home, a magnificent rainbow spanned the sky. One part of the sky was dark, cloudy, gloomy and rainy; the other in glorious sunshine. It reminded me again of the covenant love of God our Father and the hope of future glory. Life can be tough. In the gloomy darkness, we experience glimmers of light and colour which encourage us.

Death symbolised by Adam (21,22) is inevitable, because of sin. But eternal life is equally certain for those trusting in Jesus who lives today, having overcome death, the last enemy. We are privileged to be included among 'his people' (23). And *no one* need be excluded, *great* news available to the *whole* world. How can we keep that good news to ourselves? It needs to be shared with those around us.

Have you grasped what this means for *how* you live? What about also taking a step towards sharing that good news with someone you know?

DAY 80: DON'T BE SHAKEN

What feelings emerge in you when someone close dies? Grief? Guilt? Self-pity? Rage against God? Peace?

1 Corinthians 15:35-58

A dear friend, a local pastor, died while we were working in Mauritius. Full of energy and charisma, our children loved him greatly. According to custom, the body was laid out in state in his home, dressed in his best clothes. We visited next morning, afraid of how the lifeless body might affect our daughter who was under five. We need not have worried. The instant she saw him, she said: 'Père Ignace is not here. He's gone to heaven to be with Jesus!' A child's insight often astounds us.

I have read today's passage countless times at funerals, in crematoria, in church, the casket and the body a vivid reminder of our human mortality. Attempting to answer the unanswerable, Paul talks first of the unique 'bodies' of various parts of creation (36-41), turning then to the first Adam (45). He says we will have bodies in heaven but they will be different (41,42). The spiritual body (44) will be preferable to the physical one and its problems (43) which should prevent us from worrying about keeping young. This body won't last but our new one will be indestructible. A surprise may be around the corner (52). It would pay to be well prepared.

We need not fear death — death is a friend to be welcomed, allowing us to begin a new kind of existence (54). Like Wesley, we should work each day as though it is our last, knowing that 'everything we do for him is worthwhile' (58).

Can this knowledge revolutionise your everyday life and responsibilities? If you knew you were to die today, how would you spend the day? Make this your pattern for your day, anyway.

Check point

THE LIFESTYLE OF THE WISE

INTRODUCTION TO READINGS 81–95

These readings, both Old and New Testament, belong to the type of writing known as 'Wisdom'. This takes seriously each person's responsibility to listen to advice from those who have lived before, and to pass it on to those coming after us. John Donne's famous essay 'No man is an island' picks this up. The journey of life is always travelled in company, including the company of those who have gone before. It involves the journey of finding that we are people of worth, and working with others to build and sustain community.

The New Testament readings frame 'Wisdom' as 'life in Christ'. Like Wisdom, the advice for living in community is based on knowing that God is 'good' — those called by his name should live in ways that reflect this goodness. These writers also recognise that human beings find it impossible to make the right choices by themselves, but need to be transformed by God.

All of this advice is not aimed at presenting us with a checklist to line up against, or a series of rules to constantly worry about, but rather it indicates direction. God's ideal is for us to live in society, to help and sustain each other and to have travelling companions through the adventure of life. Society, like any relationship, needs working on to be built up. God's transforming presence is there for all, and we can best witness to this by the way we live together.

[The saint] strives to practice virtue heroically, not in order to be known as a virtuous and holy man, but in order that the goodness of God may never be obscured by any selfish act of his.

*(Thomas Merton, **Life and Holiness**, Palm Publishers, 1963)*

DAY 81: WISDOM AND JUSTICE

'From these [Proverbs], an ordinary person can learn to be wise,and young people can gain knowledge and good sense.'

(Proverbs 1:4)

Recall one or two proverbs you know.
What fresh insights do they offer you?

Proverbs 6:1-19

God intends human beings to live in community. Living with others always involves learning how to keep a balance between respecting others and respecting ourselves.

The 'wise' way of living builds community while recognising the worth of all people and of all creation. Today's reading is quite specific. It advises on money matters (1-5), laziness (6-11) and trouble-making (12-19). All three areas are seen to be significant in community life. Care in money matters implies having a sense of responsibility. In this age of easy credit, we can be tempted into living beyond our means. Laziness implies that some in the community are not pulling their weight, thus placing an unfair burden on others. We need to assess whether we are ignoring our specific responsibilities. Liars and trouble-makers cause break-downs in community life; the writer implies that destroying community is on a par with murder (17). In what ways might we be destroying community?

Living in harmony with others means working positively to create a healthy community. Acting responsibly in small, everyday matters is the first step towards this.

How responsible are you in the small things of life? Take time to 'audit' your actions. Do they reflect God's desire for healthy community? What new steps could you take to renew or change your patterns of life?

DAY 82: FLIRTING WITH FOLLY

*'Hidden God, whose wisdom compels our love
and unsettles all our values:
fill us with desire to search for her truth,
that we may transform the world,
becoming fools for her sake, through Jesus Christ,
your Word and Wisdom made flesh,
to whom be glory forever. Amen.'*

(The Anglican Church of Australia, ***A Prayer Book for Australia****)*

Proverbs 7:6-23

Ms Wisdom (often depicted as a woman in Proverbs) invites the young man to listen and learn from her. In contrast, Madam Folly sets out to seduce young people into 'the good life' that seems attractive, but which will lead to destruction in the end.

The picture of the unfaithful wife is used here as an allegory of any temptation to live a life that does not respect other people or ourselves. It is a powerful picture, because it recognises that the family revolves around the marriage relationship, and community revolves around the family. If trust is broken within a marriage by either partner, the family relationship crumbles. Likewise, if communal trust and respect are lacking, people become suspicious and mistrustful, community relationships fragment and life is destroyed, not affirmed.

This reading suggests that trust and fidelity are basic to life and growth — not only between marriage partners, but between all human beings. The picture presented in this passage verges on caricature. It shows a silly, irresponsible action leading eventually to death. Life is something that must be chosen and worked at. It is built up with the help and encouragement of others. To fail to put effort into building relationships is the equivalent of choosing death (as our last reading makes clear in chapter 6 verses 6-11).

Who are the people you trust most? Why do you trust them? Do they remind you more of Madam Folly or of Ms Wisdom (read Proverbs chapter 8)?

DAY 83: ON THE ROAD

'For it is one thing to see the land of peace from a wooded ridge ... and another to tread the road that leads to it.'

(Augustine)

Proverbs 13:1 — 14:8

This series of sayings encourages those who walk the road of life to prepare carefully.

The idea of life as a journey comes in 14:8, the climax of this section. Imagine setting out on a long, difficult journey without adequate preparation. You are asking for trouble! In Hebrew society, as in many other cultures, older people were expected to share their wisdom with those younger, to help prepare them for the journey of life.

This travel guide begins by pointing out that it is a good idea to choose travelling companions carefully. 'Going around with fools' (20) is a sure way to make life more difficult than necessary. On the other hand, spending time with wise friends aids our growth, and helps give us resources we can call on for the more difficult parts of the journey.

Once on the journey with good travelling companions, all aspects of life still need attention. Without this positive nurturing, life will fall into rootless wanderings. Obedience to God is the main guiding principle. To live according to this principle, whether dealing with justice, family nurture and discipline, or through sensible and honest speech, is the key to how we should continue to search for wisdom along the road of life.

Draw a graph of your life so far, showing the high points and low points. Who was with you in the high points? What helped you come through the low spots? Spend time thinking about the people with whom you share your life's journey. How can you be a 'wise friend' to them?

DAY 84: BEING 'REAL'

'But if we say we love God and don't love each other, we are liars. We can't see God. So how can we love God, if we don't love the people we can see? The commandment that God has given us is: "Love God and love each other!"' *(1 John 4:20-21)*

Proverbs 26:22 — 27:6

To live wisely is to live as a 'real' person, to be honest and open with others, comfortable enough 'in your skin' not to need defences built of pretence.

While most of the passage speaks of rather negative human behaviour, it does celebrate human life. Verse 23 highlights this. The clay pot was the most basic of domestic appliances. However, without it life would be infinitely harder. Therefore it is an object of worth, despite its humble appearance. To cover it over with a cheap glaze not only tries to pretend that it is something else, it also denies the worth of what it actually is. So smooth talking, rather than plain speaking detracts from our true self.

The main message in this passage is: Watch your words! To try to pretend you are something different through using pretentious language to 'keep up appearances', or being insincere in your comments, is destructive both of yourself and to community. Each person has worth, and believing in your own value allows you to be healthily independent of other people's opinions.

Pray this prayer, and spend some time thinking about what it may be saying to you:
'Lord, our God, our Creator, Redeemer, and Sanctifier: we ask you to cleanse us from all hypocrisy, to unite us to our fellow men and women by the bonds of peace and love, and to confirm us in holiness; now and forever, Amen.'

(The Anglican Church of Australia, ***A Prayer Book for Australia****)*

DAY 85: THE TIME OF YOUR LIFE?

'Without the help of the Lord
it is useless to build a home or to guard a city.
It is useless to get up early and stay up late
in order to earn a living.
God takes care of his own, even while they sleep.'

(Psalm 127:1-2)

Ecclesiastes 3:1-8

For the writer of Ecclesiastes (often called 'the Preacher'), the main question about life, the Universe, and everything is: 'Does life have any meaning at all?'

The Preacher speaks movingly of his life-long search for wisdom. Part of his search is to simply watch the regular patterns of life as they are played out in his world. This writer is a realist who concludes that certain patterns come around in all aspects of life. In the face of this inevitability it is foolish to try to live 'against the grain'. Being in harmony with the patterns of life, recognising that times of hope appear as regularly as times of despair, is the way to wisdom.

This passage reminds us that life consists of darkness as well as light. We are encouraged to live with both darkness and light. For the Preacher, expending energy in a constant search for deeper meaning in life is a waste of time. Life is a whole bundle of experiences, some good and some bad, but all part of the deal.

Find a place to sit outside. For 15 minutes, simply *be* in that place. See how many different sounds you can hear, scents you can smell. Feel the sun or wind on your skin. Feel yourself part of life in this place at this time. Feel God's presence in the sounds, scents and sun or wind.

DAY 86: REAL LIFE

Think of an event where you experienced happiness and peace. Close your eyes and imagine yourself there again. Imagine God there with you as the best and most understanding companion you could possibly have.

Ecclesiastes 3:9-22

This is a difficult passage with the Preacher seeing God in terms that you may find offensive or alien. God, he says, puts order into creation and gives human beings the desire to search for order while making it impossible for this desire to be fulfilled (11). Even worse, God appears to test us simply to remind us that we are no better than animals (18).

What sort of God does this reveal to us? One who treats us like an experiment, setting us up for failure! It is certainly a different picture from that of Proverbs where God is found in the goodness and order of creation.

For the writer of Ecclesiastes, goodness and order in creation may exist at times, but often life is simply not found to be good or ordered. The Preacher refuses to allow his experience of reality to be covered up by generally-accepted religious clichés. If life seems frustrating and meaningless, he insists on saying so!

This passage helps keep a balance in the presentation of religious experience. Some know God closely and intimately, and through his presence find order and meaning in life. For others who are living honest, godly lives, God feels distant and life is found to be constantly difficult. This writer finds and encourages dignity because of the way he accepts different experiences of God and life.

Where does God seem to be at the moment for you? Near or far? Clear, or hidden behind a barrier? Wherever and however you experience God, accept that this is a legitimate part of your Christian journey.

DAY 87: ENJOY LIFE, AND BE WISE

'You are like a letter written by Christ... But you aren't written with pen and ink or on tablets made of stone. You are written in our hearts by the Spirit of the living God.'

(2 Corinthians 3:3)

Ecclesiastes 9:7-16

If God seems so distant, and life is so meaningless (see our last reading), why bother even trying to live good lives? Why bother living at all?

The Preacher insists that life itself is full of pleasure. The simple acts of eating and drinking bring joy. Yet we can run around in circles trying to find even more pleasure or meaning, ignoring what is under our nose. Simple pleasures can be found anywhere by those who look for them.

Eating and drinking are communal activities. Happiness is found in time spent with friends and loved ones. Work is to be enjoyed for its own sake, not for money or status; its results are beyond our control (11).

Using the picture of life as a journey, this writer encourages us to enjoy each small step of the journey for its own sake. Spending life hurrying towards some desired destination, he says, is a foolish waste of time. We cannot know the destination, and if our eyes are fixed ahead, we fail to see and enjoy the simple gifts of life along the way. To live fully in each moment, savouring the pleasure of company, work, food and drink, is to live wisely.

Write a list of the activities you enjoy most. Imagine yourself sitting at Jesus' feet, telling him about some of these activities, and thanking him for the gift of simple times of enjoyment.

DAY 88: TRANSFORMED LIVING

Can you think of a particular defining moment or incident in your life that turned your thinking around? What was it and why was it important to you?

Romans 12:1-21

When you read that you should offer yourself up to God as a 'living sacrifice' (1) what does that suggest to you? Images of 'holy war' have become etched on our minds through our TV screens as fanatical nationalists sacrifice themselves for various causes in fiery and violent self-immolations, believing they will be transported immediately into Paradise. But Paul here is encouraging us to lead full and disciplined lifestyles, rather than expecting us to take his remarks literally. We are to let God transform our thoughts and actions (2) rather than allow ourselves to be taken in by current fads and thinking.

When we let our differing gifts and abilities be used, the whole community benefits (4-8). We should aim at the best in all we do (9), caring also for one another (10), persevering in spiritual matters (11). Caring for those in need or giving hospitality to those whose paths cross ours (12,13) should become second nature to us.

Paul gives good advice for everyday living. Life is to be shared with those around us, both good and bad times (15). We are to regard ourselves as part of our neighbourhood, not above it (16) and if someone hurts us it is up to God to take revenge, not us (14,17-20).

If you are unaware of your particular abilities, ask God's Spirit to reveal them to you, then talk about your particular strengths with Christian friends or someone you trust (4-8). And when you know them, continue to open yourself up to new possibilities for service and 'let God change the way you think' (2).

DAY 89: LOVE IN ACTION

Ugandan bishop Festo Kivengere scandalised the world with his little book, *I Love Idi Amin*. Fleeing for his life, his archbishop Janani Luwum cruelly martyred by Amin, untold thousands butchered, still Festo could write what he did. He really meant it. How come?

Romans 13:1-14

Today's passage tells us how we should live in society. Believers are expected to obey their rulers (1-7) and pay their dues (8-10; cf. John 13:34, James 4:7-10). Life here is temporary and we must prepare for Christ's return (11-14). Obeying (5) and paying taxes (6), is not without exception (see Acts 5:29).

Our loving God is the source of all authority, so we should play our part as dependable members of society. As salt and light, we have a responsibility to influence society for good and for God, primarily through the quality of our lives and how the love we show to our neighbour is measured (9).

Paul touches on our motivation for right living. It should not be from fear of God's anger (5) — even though we and others of our generation should be aware of that reality (13)! Rather it should be because God's love prompts us to keep the Law (10). The 'do not's' of the ten commandments get a bad press today (9), seen as too restricting. Passages like verses 8-10 can be misused to give permission for all kinds of behaviour unacceptable to a holy God. Even superficial analysis shows the rules are clearly designed for our wellbeing. Finally, our motivation should include preparing for the unexpected coming of our Lord (11,12). We never know what a new day brings. Beware!

Light, whether it's a torch or natural daylight, exposes what we thought may have been hidden. Does verse 12 fill you with encouragement or embarrassment?

DAY 90: MIND YOUR OWN BUSINESS!

Many of us have friends with strong views on food, drink or behaviour, such as vegetarians, reformed smokers or recovered alcoholics. Some make us feel guilty? Why do we find them difficult to get along with? Is it self-righteousness, arrogance or their criticism hitting home? How important are the issues?

Romans 14:1-23

Christians can be as critical and judgmental as the rest of the community. Divisions within the church, even those resulting from a passion for truth or justice, must grieve the heart of God 'who welcomes everyone' (3). Heresy, immorality or wrong behavior should be disciplined appropriately, but here Paul suggests we focus too much on inconsequentials like eating or worship habits. Too often we assume that people whose lifestyle or beliefs are different to ours must be wrong.

'Mind your own business!' Paul says (4). Each of us personally is accountable to God (5). We should therefore follow the 'stumbling-block principle', and aim to do nothing to cause another to stumble in their faith journey because of our eating, drinking or habits (21). What does matter is whether our lifestyle pleases God, bringing about peace and happiness (17). A good principle is: 'If in doubt, don't!', which should also include not compromising our beliefs (23). We need to develop a faith with 'backbone', which is not easily swayed by the latest fads of belief or behaviour. But also, keep your reasons for doing so or not, to yourself (22). And work peacefully and help each another (19) rather than criticising and judging those who differ from you.

Paul tells us to live at peace with and help each other (19). Who have you criticised or judged, even with good reason? What steps could you take to accept them as openly as God does?

DAY 91: ONCE BITTEN, TWICE SHY

It's no fun being let down. You feel angry or stupid. As you read, you may feel sympathetic towards Paul's friend, Philemon.

Philemon

In the courts recently, a convicted American criminal fought a decision to deport him from Australia as an undesirable alien for a crime he committed 30 years ago. When is the line crossed between having to keep paying for our sin, and being freed from its penalty?

Onesimus had apparently cheated Philemon (18) who probably hoped his slave had gone for good. But Paul pleads for a second chance for him (17) now that he has found faith. He writes diplomatically, cajoling, persuading, pleading with Philemon, presumably afraid he will not be positive towards taking Onesimus back. As a Christian, the church leader Philemon (2) would have experienced the sense of being forgiven in Christ. We twitch when we catch ourselves saying the Lord's Prayer, 'forgive us ... as we forgive others...' (Matthew 6:9-14).

Paul not only encouraged Philemon to take Onesimus back but to begin treating him in a totally differently way. He clearly trusted him now, and was prepared to stand behind the converted slave, covering the costs of any debts he might have incurred (18,19). But more than that, he urged him to start a new relationship with him, no longer as a slave but as a brother in Christ. It is a striking model of how Christians are to live, with no barriers of race, class or gender (Galatians 3:28). That is still hard to do in practice.

Is there a person who has betrayed you in some way who you still find difficult to forgive? In the light of this passage, what do you think Paul would advise you to do?

DAY 92: NOURISHING RELATIONSHIPS

What marks a good relationship? Give and take for a start. Today, much is made of rights in relationships rather than the need for selfless love. The more we demand our rights, the less we experience lasting love. The creativity needed involves being proactive and practical in loving without becoming a doormat for others to trample on!

Ephesians 5:21-33

Have you found the key to nourishing relationships, including marriage? Verse 21 puts it succinctly — putting the other person first. And in the case of Christian marriage — honouring Christ. Left to our own ideas, we might be tempted to assert domination and authority. After all, effective leadership today requires a touch of aggression, so they say! Instead, Jesus has shown us self-giving servanthood. As members of the Church, we benefit by his willingness to give his life for us (25). That's the Christian model for success. It's a mystery really (32).

Jesus' dream is for a holy church, spotless and wrinkle-free (27) as they say in the laundry detergent ads! How could anyone be that perfect? Impossible without Christ's self-giving. Likewise a marriage relationship can hope to be 'wrinkle-free' only through self-giving love. Giving and receiving, rather than demanding. It actually comes down to very practical things … in the heat of the moment and after a tough day! Perhaps the hardest words to say are 'I'm sorry; I was wrong; I love you'.

Have you ever observed tense couples shopping in a supermarket? Seen the expression on the faces, heard the tone of voice? You can almost see the statistics of marriage breakdown spiralling upwards! And the same can be seen in church meetings too! What kind of glue is needed in your own closest relationships? Try noting the ingredients on a scrap of paper now.

DAY 93: MAKING RELATIONSHIPS WORK

Think about a parent/child tension or an employer/employee conflict you have seen or experienced. What would make a difference?

Ephesians 6:1-9

All children push the boundaries of behaviour when finding what is acceptable to their parents. Finding their identity and independence can be a painful process for all involved! We all will have experienced some aspect of conflict between the generations. Here, Paul gives straightforward advice for families (1-4) based on mutual respect.

At least two parties are involved in relationships, and each bears some responsibility for how they work. The relationship between parent and child is complicated. Many factors contribute to conflict situations. Parents may be:

- imposing their authority to prove they are in charge
- imitating the model their parents gave them
- afraid their child will be harmed
- suffering from sheer exhaustion!

It is hard to change our habits to better ways of parenting. So it is with employer-employee relationships. Imagine being a union representative if both labour and management heeded verses 5-9! Mention of slaves jars the twentieth century ear, even though they were an accepted part of first-century life. But similar relationship principles still apply today: workers are to serve as if they are serving the Lord, though they may have to stretch their imaginations a little! And employers need to realise we are all equal at the foot of the Cross. One day each of us will have to account for the way we have treated those who have served us (9).

Imagine you are prescribing an antidote for the irritations between parents and children or between workers and bosses. What would the 'serum' comprise?

DAY 94: FAMILY RESPONSIBILITIES

Widows are not a modern phenomenon! Men tend to die earlier than women. Glance around your local church or retirement village for confirmation. Who make up the majority of passengers on bus tours or luxury cruises?

1 Timothy 5:3-16

In Paul's time, widows presented a serious social problem, especially if they had no family. They became outcasts of society. Nor did everyone in the church accept their responsibilities, for some widows had family who were not caring for them, and others no family at all. Guidelines were therefore needed. The principles for the church are clear: widows in genuine need are to be looked after (3) but the primary responsibility is within the family itself (4). There are harsh words for families who do not take care of their relatives (8).

In Africa and Polynesia, where I have worked, there are no such institutions as old peoples' homes. It is taken for granted that old folk are cared for by the family. They are cherished and respected. There is a disturbing trend in our Western society to view the elderly as cast-offs. Economic rationalists ask whether our system can afford to care for them. But the old and widowed have so much to offer. In the church, many have a strategic ministry of prayer. They are often the ones who take a special interest in the young. One day you will join their ranks. How would you like to be treated?

Plan to spend time with an elderly person and make it a regular event. Draw them out, asking leading questions to discover something of their life story. When you are unsure how to act, put yourself in their situation each time, treating them as you would like yourself to be treated.

DAY 95: RESPECT YOUR ELDERS

Some families have 'roast preacher' for Sunday lunch! They criticise the sermon or service in a destructive way. When I was a teenager, a friend presented our new minister with a four page critique of his first sermon! Poor man.

1 Timothy 5:17 — 6:2

Life is tough for ministers today. Being human, of course there will be something to criticise. Many people find the church is irrelevant and think the minister or priest works for only a couple of hours on Sunday. Secular specialists have taken over many of the tasks that used to be part of ministry, creating a crisis of identity for many in ministry. So even church members begin to doubt whether their minister is worth the pay (18).

The unrelenting demands of ministry play havoc with the mental and spiritual well-being with them and if they are married, with family life. The burnout rate is horrifying, with approximately 10,000 former ministers in Australia alone! Inadequate preparation for ministry is only some of the problem (22). A major contributing factor may stem from feeling not needed or unwanted, of being irrelevant or unappreciated.This can sometimes leads to behaviour which betrays the high calling of the ministry (20).

Each member of a church has an important role to perform. We can encourage and pray faithfully for our ministers. In a very real sense, we get the pastoral care we deserve but they *can* become the ministers we long to have.

List criticisms you feel about your pastors. Transform them one by one into a prayer so that God may transform your criticisms into something positive. Find a way of offering non-patronising encouragement to your ministers.

LIVING IN THE LIGHT OF THE FUTURE

INTRODUCTION TO READINGS 96–100

Christians have been described as living in the tension between the 'already' and the 'not yet'. We experience salvation through Christ, but still live in an imperfect world in which 'all creation is still groaning and is in pain' (Romans 8:22).

Paul provides comfort to the early Christians, many of whom were suffering persecution for their faith, by reminding them that this gap between present tense and future perfect is filled by the comforting work of the Spirit.

Paul's letters to the churches at Philippi and Thessalonika reflect this ongoing struggle. The imagery of a marathon is apt; it requires training and dedication to be completed, but is well worth the pain when the prize is won. To the Thessalonians, he reminds them of Jesus' promise to return. He cautions that this is cause for hope, not for useless speculation about times and places. Life is to be lived in the light of hope, rather than in the darkness of despair.

Similarly, the Book of Revelation addresses a situation in which many Christians were being martyred, and despair was rife among small, struggling communities who asked where hope lay.

John uses a type of writing called 'Apocalyptic' to address these concerns. This is the writing of the oppressed underground; carefully coded to have meaning only to those 'in the know', it stresses the power of God over and above human history, to make all things new and to vindicate his people's faithfulness. Much time has been spent trying to decode the images in this book, but we simply don't have the 'inside' knowledge for much of it. What we do have is the beauty and power of pictorial language and the sense of the greatness and saving grace of God, who continues in faithfulness through all time, and whose faithfulness we are encouraged to match.

DAY 96: RIGHT THERE WITH YOU

'There's light at the end of the tunnel.' Is that light at the end of your tunnel a sunny morning or an oncoming train? Are you feeling hopeful or fearful? Talk to God about your difficulties and watch for reassurance as you read on.

Romans 8:12-27

There are as many causes of human suffering as there are human beings. Paul lists some of them: unfulfilled desires (12,13) which cause bitterness and dissatisfaction; fear of God (15), perhaps because of sin and guilt; confusion (20); growing awareness of our mortality (21); pain of all kinds (22) — physical, spiritual, and psychological. When we can't seem to get in touch with God (26) it can be excruciatingly painful and frustrating. God's Spirit prays for us (26). Our gracious God does not leave us in our abyss of pain.

- We can relate with God like children in a personal way — trusting, dependent, loved and forgiven (16).
- God will keep his promises (17), unlike many parents who make threats and promises but rarely keep them.
- However bad our suffering is now (18), when we experience what God has prepared for his children, it will suddenly seem like nothing.
- God assures us about our future (23) in the long term, even if not in the here and now. Waiting will have its fair share of pain (17,18,22,23), but freedom will come (21,23).
- We are not alone. Although we are weak, vulnerable and defenceless (26), the Spirit of God comes alongside us to strengthen us in our weakness.

Search this passage for reassurances from God about difficulties and suffering. Note them — for pressure you're facing now, or for future reference.

DAY 97: WHAT I REALLY WANT IS . . .

Have you heard the old song 'All I want for Christmas is my two front teeth'? What would you give your two front teeth for; what do you want most in the world?

Philippians 3:2-16

When your defences are down, what matters most to you? For Paul, his Jewish heritage really mattered (4) and his strict legalism made him feel accepted by God (6).

But then a life-changing experience turned those values on their head. He even called his former values garbage (8). Now it was a living friendship with the Messiah that mattered more than anything else to him. To know and be reassured that he belonged to Christ was of paramount importance to him (9). None of his previous record had ever been able to provide that. Previously, all the initiative for the relationship had come from Paul; now the initiative was God's ['God accepted me...' (9); 'Christ has taken hold of me...' (12); 'this is the prize that God offers because of what Christ Jesus has done' (14)].

You would think such a prize would be highly desirable, a source of pleasure. Highly desirable maybe, but what Paul most wanted was a chance to share in his Lord's suffering and death (10) so that he could also share in his resurrection. For him, this was no easy gospel. Already in jail, Paul was part way towards achieving his goal. He had no intention of giving up the race as a lost cause(12). Perseverence, tenacity, commitment, single-mindedness and courage describe Paul's faith journey. 'All of us ... should think in this same way' (15) he urges.

How would you describe your journey as a Christian? A sprint? A marathon? An obstacle course? An uphill climb?

DAY 98: ULTIMATE CERTAINTIES

When I was a child, a great amphitheatre was built nearby for spectators to view the second coming of Christ who was expected to appear through the heads of Sydney Harbour! Realism replaced expectations and today a block of apartments is there. The theologians call the second coming the 'Parousia'. But is it a lot of baloney?

1 Thessalonians 4:13 — 5:11

The early Christians believed Jesus was returning very soon. They had been well taught (5:2) but were worried about loved ones who had already died. What would happen to them? The clear answer is they will be saved on the basis of faith in Jesus (14).

TV producers of live programs prepare a 'running sheet' with all elements, timed to the second so that everyone involved knows exactly what to expect. There is no such Bible 'running sheet' to predict the Parousia. It may be vague about detail, but the certainty of the event itself is not vague at all. It will be the climax of the world's history as we know it. It may came as a surprise, but it will surely happen. Come to think of it, the first coming of Jesus was somewhat of a surprise to those living at the time!

Why does the Bible include this teaching? To scare the living daylights out of us? (Note in verse 16 that the event will surprise 'the living daylights' *into* those already dead!) There is one major reason for this teaching about the future. It is so we will live our lives to be always ready for Christ and will do what Christ wants us to do. In contrast to learning from the past, we are here encouraged to learn from the future. Do you ever encourage another Christians to live like this?

DAY 99: REDEEMED HUMANITY

Have you ever attended a large Christian gathering of people of many nationalities? What drew you together? Maybe a taste of heaven? John, the writer of revelation gives a sense of this indescribable experience. Everyone complete, everyone whole. God, not us at the centre.

Revelation 7:9-17

John has just described symbolically the biblical completion of the twelve tribes of Israel (4). Now he paints a scene of every race, tribe, nation and language (9) gathered together around the throne of heaven. All human barriers are broken down, racism now non-existent. Any traces of tears will be wiped away once and for all (17) and the symbols of human suffering, 'white robes' (9,13,14) and 'palm branches' (9) representing victory over suffering, become the focus.

Many believers still suffer for their faith. Recently I read of a 14-year-old Pakistani Christian girl who was abducted and forced to convert; leaders of a church in Bogotà, Colombia, attacked; Ethiopian believers seriously injured by a mob; members of a church in Mexico told to deny their faith or leave town; Russian laws restricting believers' rights; Nepalis oppressed by Hindu nationalism. This should not surprise us (14), but it is not the end of the story. One day, suffering will disappear (16) and we will experience the protectiveness of a merciful and gracious God (15). Sadness will give way to pure bliss (17). The focus of attention will be on the worship of God (15), turning from us and our needs to the Lamb who is the shepherd (17), who has promised to provide all we need.

In the light of this, how can we best prepare for our life with God? What should be our attitude to suffering — ours and others?

DAY 100: WELL WORTH THE WAIT!

Perhaps *the* highlight of my life was a visit to Jerusalem where I preached in the Garden Tomb at the Easter sunrise service. With hundreds of people from all over the world, then walking the streets of the old city to retrace the steps Jesus walked, it was a deeply emotional experience. John describes the new Jerusalem here, saying this is way beyond anything he could accurately describe.

Revelation 21:9 — 22:5

It is tempting to read into symbols, but that shouldn't prevent your imagination feeling, seeing, touching and smelling as John attempts to describe the indescribable. Certain features stand out: dazzling, clear brightness (11), a stark contrast to the dirt and pollution of today's cities; a sense of vastness (16); beauty and variety as represented by the precious stones (19-21); life and healing, symbolised by the river and the constantly changing fruit trees (22:2).

But these striking features are not the focus of John's vision. He focuses on God and the Lamb, and their shared relationship to be enjoyed by all who have trusted Jesus. The battle won on the Cross is fulfilled. The enemy and his followers have no place in the new Jerusalem. God's curses no longer have hold (30). Darkness, sin and fear will never again be present (5). All human attempts to contain and control God in churches, temples or institutions, are absent (21:22). Yet *the* church ('the bride and wife of the Lamb', 21:9), is the glory of God, who proudly shows her to John in all her splendour (10).

What is life at the End for you? A big question mark or the anticipation of a huge party? How would you help your church get ready? And live it *today?*

Light for the path

HAVE YOU SEEN THIS SIGN BEFORE? THE SCRIPTURE UNION LOGO IS A LAMP - A STYLISED VERSION OF THE CLAY LAMPS OF THE TIME OF JESUS.

This logo can be seen all around the world (see opposite page). It was chosen to express the theme of Psalm 119 verse 105. 'Your word is a lamp to guide me'. Scripture Union wants to help people read the Bible. A torch or a street lamp helps us to see our way in the dark. So reading the Bible helps us to see the way to live in the world.

Foothold is one of Scripture Union's Bible resources. This introduces you to the whole range of Bible guides designed to suit people of all stages and ages.

But publishing Bible guides is not the only way Scripture Union workers try to open the Bible's message with people. Staff and trained volunteers can be found amongst school children, in holiday camps, sharing God's good news wherever kids gather in suburban centres and at holiday resorts. Scripture Union workers operate in partnership with local churches and community groups.

If you would like to find out more about Scripture Union's activities, programs and other resources contact your nearest Scripture Union office. The address is on the opposite page. Just mention *Foothold* when you write.

And keep watching this sign. You never know where you will see it next!

WHERE TO FIND

Scripture Union

AUSTRALIA: PO Box 2915, Fitzroy DC, Victoria 3065

CANADA: 1885 Clements Road, Unit 226, Pickering, Ontario L1W 3V4

ENGLAND & WALES: 207-209 Queensway, Bletchley, Milton Keynes, Bucks MK2 2EB, England

FIJI: PO Box 1278, Suva

HONG KONG: St Andrew's Centre, 138 Nathan Road, Kowloon

NEW ZEALAND: PO Box 760, Wellington

NORTHERN IRELAND: 157 Albertbridge Road, Belfast BT5 4PS

PAPUA NEW GUINEA: PO Box 280, University, NCD

PENINSULAR MALAYSIA: 386 Jalan 5/59, 46000 Petaling Jaya, Selangor

PHILIPPINES: PO Box 4442, Manila CPO 1099

SABAH: PO Box 11419, 88815 Kota Kinabalu

SARAWAK: PO Box 1099, 83722 Kuching

SCOTLAND: 9 Canal Street, Glasgow G4 OAB

SINGAPORE: #03-07, 7 Armenian Street, Singapore 179932

SOLOMON ISLANDS: PO Box 294, Honiara

SOUTH AFRICA: PO Box 291, Rondebosch 7701, Cape Town

THAILAND: 800/100-102 Dragoon Sul Lane, Asoke-Dindaeng Road, Bangkok 10400

TONGA: PO Box 825, Nuku'alofa

USA: Suite 215, 150 Strafford Avenue, Wayne, PA 19087

VANUATU: PO Box 379, Port Vila

WESTERN SAMOA: PO Box 2890, Apia

INTERNATIONAL OFFICE: 207 - 209 Queensway, Bletchley, Milton Keynes, Bucks MK2 2EB, England